THE
SCHOLAR
GYPSY

'The Scholar-Gypsy having given them an account of
the necessity, which drove him to that kind of life, told
them, that the people he went with were not such imposters
as they were taken for, but that they had a traditional kind
of learning among them, and could do wonders by the
power of imagination, and that [he] himself had learnt
much from their art, and improved it further than
[they] themselves could.'

Joseph Glanvill, 'The Scholar-Gypsy', 1661

John Sampson by Augustus John, c. 1903

THE
SCHOLAR
GYPSY

The Quest for a Family Secret

ANTHONY SAMPSON

JOHN MURRAY
Albemarle Street, London

First published in 1997
by John Murray (Publishers) Ltd.,
50 Albemarle Street, London W1X 4BD

A catalogue record for this book is available from the British Library

ISBN 0-7195-5708-9

Typeset in Palatino 11/14 pt by Anneset
Weston-super-Mare, Somerset

Printed and bound in Great Britain by
The University Press, Cambridge

For Dorothy and John,
my sister and brother,
who shared the puzzle

Contents

Illustrations

1

The Silence

AS A CHILD I had only a hazy memory of my grandfather John Sampson. Not long before he died in 1931, when I was aged 5, he came to stay with us in Hampstead for the wedding of my aunt Honor: I can still visualize a formidable but magical old man with a big bald head and strong chin, who played with us in the garden. But after his death his spirit seemed to hover as a shadow over both my parents.

My mother would sometimes talk about him with a dread which could only fascinate a child – about his ferocious temper, his heavy drinking, his wicked but unstated habits, and about a woman in Liverpool, 'the wretched Dora', who apparently stood between him and our family. Yet our house also contained relics which provided more attractive clues, including a fine romantic drawing of him by Augustus John and another of a gypsy gazing at a seductive girl; a book of gypsy folktales; and a daunting Oxford dictionary of the Romani language, compiled by John Sampson.

That gypsy hinterland naturally aroused the curiosity of a child. My mother told me how the gypsies called my grandfather 'the Rai', the gentleman or scholar. But my father was always reluctant to talk about him – or anyone else for that matter – for he was a reticent man who found fulfilment in his work as a scientist and retreated into silence at home. My child's instinct sensed there was something unresolved in our background which separated us from less reserved families.

As I grew into my teens I began to feel this tension more strongly: that the family was under a curse for which the mysterious Rai was somehow responsible. He seemed to hold a spell over anyone who had known him, to be always linked with those mysterious gypsies. Yet his memory in the family seemed to have gone up in smoke, like a caravan at a gypsy funeral. And the travellers' world itself – the brightly painted horse-drawn wagons on lonely roads, the wild-haired musicians playing round camp-fires – was being obliterated by the relentless expansion of suburbs and motor cars, or tamely imitated by Boy Scout camps and mass-produced caravans.

Among the relics of my grandfather in our house I came across a folder full of yellowed press cuttings. They told of his funeral on a Welsh mountain and conjured up a bright vision of that vanished world and his own part in it, and of intense friendships and loyalties which raised all kinds of questions. From them I pieced together the strange story which in 1931 had briefly dominated the headlines of the popular papers.

They told how on the morning of 21 November an extraordinary gathering of mourners converged on the small Welsh village of Llangwm just below Foel Goch, the 'Red Mountain', where my grandfather had asked for his ashes

The front page of the Daily Mirror, *23 November 1931*

to be scattered. The mourners included my father and an odd mixture of gypsies and scholars, the former Lord Mayor of Liverpool, the painter Augustus John and one woman, my grandfather's academic assistant Dora Yates.

As one journalist described the scene:

On an open space in the street was a motley crew indeed. Farm hands in quaintly-cut corduroys, the representatives of Romany, rich and poor, ladies in fur coats, and gentlemen in plus fours. Seated at a harp was a dark, flashing-eyed gipsy maiden, twanging a plaintive melody, the while a white-haired member of the same tribe accompanied on the fiddle. Gipsies greeted each other in their own language, and kissed in the true gipsy fashion. It was a most picturesque scene – the male gipsies in their red bandana kerchiefs, and the fairer sex in colourful but tattered dresses, and hair bedecked with spangles and coins. Hundreds of spectators looked on and waited – waited for the coming of the last mortal remains of Dr John Sampson, the well known philologist and librarian of Liverpool University.

The odd party processed slowly up the mountain, led by the gypsy Ithal Lee bearing the casket of ashes and followed by gypsy musicians with harps, fiddles, clarinet and dulcimer. Among the musicians were three descendants of the great harpist John Roberts of Newtown – his son with a harp, his grandson with a violin and his great-grandson with a flute. Then came my father looking stiff and ill at ease, and Augustus John 'rather Gypsy-like in his full grey beard and his scarlet-spotted scarf'.

Eventually they reached a plateau of level grass just below the summit of the mountain. The sun shone in a clear blue sky and beneath them lay the Welsh valley, with the Snowdon range visible on the horizon. Augustus John stood bareheaded in the centre – 'his eyes fixed on the distance, a smouldering cigarette in his hand' – and proclaimed in a powerful voice:

Obeying his last wishes, we, his friends, bear hither the ashes of JOHN SAMPSON in order that, scattered over the slopes of this beautiful mountain, they may become part of the land he loved and rest near the remnant of the ancient race for whom he lived. We build no monument, we inscribe no stone to bear his name. Long will he live in our hearts: longer still in the great work he has done. Mourn we must that never again can we take by the hand the most faithful of friends; yet we rejoice that he was sent among us to be our companion in sorrow and in joy, to protect from decay our old traditions, and to enrich the world's store of learning.

Ithal Lee held out the casket to my father who took the ashes and scattered them nine times over the mountain-side. The mourners recited the Romani words for 'earth to earth, ashes to ashes, dust to dust'. One Welsh spectator was heard to exclaim: 'Pity 'tis to scatter the ashes so, and give the Almighty all the work of collecting them together again.' Then Augustus John stretched out his right arm and recited Romani verses that the Rai had written thirty years before.

> Scholar Gypsy, Brother, Student,
>   Peacefully I kiss thy forehead,
> Quietly I depart and leave
>   Thee whom I loved – 'Good night'. . .
>
> Across death's dark stream
>   I give thee my hand; and what
> Thou would'st have desired for thyself
>   I wish thee: May'st thou sleep well.

The mourners raised their hands and repeated the

Romani blessing: *'te soves misto'* – 'may'st thou sleep well' – and Reuben Roberts played on the heavy triple harp the Rai's favourite tune, the Welsh lament 'David of the White Rock'. Harpists and fiddlers joined in with other tunes. Ithal Lee broke up the casket and burnt it to cinders – burning the property of the dead in gypsy style – and then quietly lit his pipe from the blaze. Some mourners thought this irreverent but Ithal had always insisted that 'in his heart the Rai *was* a gypsy'; and later he confided: 'I knew the Rai would have said to me, "Aren't you going to light up, Ithal?" – you see I hadn't had a smoke all morning.'

Then the mourners and musicians turned away and walked slowly down to Llangwm. Tears were rolling down Augustus's cheeks, but the gypsies insisted that weeping and laments would disturb the rest of the dead.

Later, the gypsies, scholars and friends all reassembled for a funeral feast, complete with the best wines and cigars, a few miles away at The White Lion in the hilltop town of Cerig-y-Drudion. Marguerite Owen, the licensee, could not recall such a sumptuous feast: 'We have made great preparations such as we have never made before, nor any of our predecessors.'

The funeral was front-page news on the following Monday. The *Daily Mirror* made it their lead story – GIPSY RITES FOR ROMANY SCHOLAR – with photographs of a gypsy fiddler, my father scattering the ashes, and the mourners walking up the mountain. The *Daily Graphic* carried a page of pictures. The *Daily Telegraph* showed the fiddlers gathering round the harpist: GYPSY LAMENT ON WELSH PEAK. But after that day of fame silence descended: nothing to explain how a professor and philologist had attracted such love from those gypsy families and such a remarkable collection of mourners; no mention of why my father appeared so aloof and ill at ease among his own father's closest friends, nor why he never talked about it afterwards; nothing to explain why my grandmother was not there, nor why the only woman, Dora Yates, was unknown to the rest of us. My father's own embarrassment appears to have extended to a general dislike of journalism and publicity, which made the cuttings seem thoroughly intrusive.

And then there was another subject of embarrassment which deepened the family silence.

Soon after my grandfather died an 'Aunt Mary' came to stay with us in the holidays, a big, square-jawed schoolteacher with pebble glasses and a prim Edinburgh accent who seemed to have dropped in from another universe. She was kind to us children: she taught me chess, and how to cover the whole board with knights' moves; and she strode tirelessly among the hills reciting poetry and discussing Greek myths. But when I asked my mother how Aunt Mary fitted in with the other Sampsons, she just said: 'I'll tell you when you're older.' Not until I was 18 did she explain what I had long since guessed: that Aunt Mary was my grandfather's illegitimate daughter.

When I went to Oxford after the war, abandoning science in favour of English literature, I became more aware and proud of my grandfather's achievements. But he was a daunting ghost, with his grammarian's rigour and philological pedantry which I so patently lacked. And I was puzzled by the contradictions in his character: I could not square his dry scholarship with the seductive drawing by his friend Augustus – or with his illegitimate daughter.

After Oxford I went to Johannesburg to edit a black magazine, *DRUM*, and thus began my career as a journalist. I spent many drunken evenings in shebeens with black South African writers and politicians, relaxing in their witty camaraderie and relishing the escape from inhibited white society. Later I reflected that my grandfather might have enjoyed such escapades. He had, it was true, a much more disciplined and scholarly mind: he would have taken notes, however drunk, on Bantu grammar or inflections; and he would have disapproved of any journalist writing carelessly in order to meet deadlines. But I wondered if I had inherited some of his Bohemian genes or had subconsciously mirrored his revolt against conventions, which my father had so deplored.

Before my father died, when I was still in my twenties, he briefly opened up and spoke to me more freely. He was pleased that I had written my first book and that I might even make some sort of living out of writing. From his deathbed he wanted to tell me more family history. I felt at ease with him for the first time. But he told me nothing of Aunt Mary nor of his father's gypsy world.

It was not until I was in my sixties, now more detached from the contemporary world and more conscious of my own mortality, that I became determined to uncover the family mystery. Encouraged by my wife, sister and cousins, I began to follow up such clues to his secret life as remained. My search soon turned into an engrossing paperchase of discoveries, false trails and sudden treasure. In London I looked more carefully through the two black tin boxes in my cellar which held my grandfather's letters. In the London Library I pored over the volumes of the Gypsy Lore Society of which he had been President. In Edinburgh I made more visits to Aunt Mary, now in her eighties, to try to coax some hints from her. In North Wales I found the small village and the house on the hill where my grandfather had spent holidays pursuing his gypsy studies and young women. At the National Library of Wales at Aberystwyth I found the Augustus John archive containing many of my grandfather's best letters.

In Liverpool, where the Rai had spent most of his life, I found the most unexpected clues. His official and respectable career was handsomely commemorated by a Latin inscription in the entrance hall of the University Library over which he had ruled for nearly forty years. But the cellars of the Library revealed a much more intimate story: the well-documented Sampson archive preserved secrets which he had diligently concealed in his lifetime. One envelope held bawdy verses to his academic colleague Dora Yates which left no doubt about their true relationship. Other envelopes contained letters from his university colleagues which revealed their wild adventures behind the façades of academe. Still others disclosed bitter wrangles between the two sides of the Rai's family over his funeral and began to explain the traumas that lurked behind my father's silence. In those cellars I felt I was exorcizing a family ghost.

My search also brought to life the lost world of the rural gypsies which had so enthralled the Rai and his coterie of scholars, artists and writers a century ago. Faded letters from half-literate gypsies, sepia photographs of Romani families sitting around their caravans and tents, learned exchanges about Romani syntax and inflections, all conjured up the thrilling pursuit of the dark-skinned people who kept appearing and disappearing in the wild corners of Wales, slowly giving up the secrets of their language, and hence their origins. I began to understand the power of the gypsy spell, and the longing for an alternative society, as the last fling of the Romantic movement before the twentieth century closed in on it.

2

Scholar Gypsy

IT WAS IN Victorian Liverpool, which seemed to hold the key to the family mystery, that I began my search. I became engrossed in the task of uncovering the past glory and vitality of that great city from the clutter and decay of later generations. The bleakness of contemporary Liverpool, with its mean office blocks, its supermarkets and the raised highway that runs through the centre, has disguised its earlier grandeur. But its decline has also limited the destruction which has laid waste so many other city centres in Britain. Today the exuberant old palaces of Liverpool's waterfront still evoke the pride of one of the world's great ports, looking out over the wide river whose emptiness reveals the end of its maritime supremacy.

Liverpool was always a world apart. Wilder in character than the rest of Britain, it marked the frontier where the outlying components of the British Isles – Irish, Scots and Welsh – met England. As a seaport it had always depended on the hazards of trade. In the eighteenth century the city had grown rich on the African slave trade and, though the trade was abolished in 1807, it soon came to be replaced by the far more profitable expansion of the North Atlantic trade in passengers and goods, carrying them to and from booming New York, Baltimore and Boston. The world's first railway, from Liverpool to Manchester, built in 1830, connected the seaport with inland factories; and the transatlantic steamships and liners, beginning with Cunard's *Britannia* in 1840, brought an endless stream of cosmopolitan passengers through Europe's chief gateway to America. Every year hundreds of thousands of Europeans sailed from Liverpool; and whole communities of Germans, Dutch and Scandinavians settled in the city to profit from the transatlantic trade. By the 1860s the growth of the docks along the Mersey, with miles of quays, forests of masts and queues of sailing-ships and steamships, provided, as the French historian Hippolyte Taine wrote, 'one of the greatest spectacles of the whole world'.

It was also a city of spectacular contrasts. The chaos and squalor of nineteenth-century Liverpool became notorious as 'the black spot on the Mersey' or 'that black hole' as the American consul Nathaniel Hawthorne called it in the 1850s. The potato famine in Ireland had brought 300,000 impoverished Irish into Liverpool in one year alone, filling the streets with wretched beggars. The docks provided all kinds of unconventional jobs and opportunities, legal and illegal, regular or fitful, and attracted every variety of human flotsam and jetsam, including tinkers, mumpers – and gypsies.

By the mid-nineteenth century the richer Liverpool merchants had become much more respectable and responsible than their slave-trading forebears, planning hospitals, schools, parks and charities, and financing grandiose buildings like St George's Hall, the Walker Art Gallery and the Picton Library which today still give classical pomp to the city centre. But the more prosperous citizens were already moving out of the Georgian terraces of Toxteth into the suburbs; and the municipal palaces were never far from poverty and squalor. For miles up the Mersey you could see, wrote one observer, 'a continuous dense mass of houses, over which there hangs for ever a dense pall of dun-coloured smoke, visible on clear days from many miles distance'. All round the sprawling dockyards starving children begged in the streets and drunken sailors brawled in the pubs which proliferated in Liverpool as nowhere else. The contrast between rich and poor was shocking to visitors from the south of England. In 1884 *The Times* described 'the hordes of the ragged and the wretched men and women in the cruellest grip of poverty, little children with shoeless feet, bodies pinched', while 'the superb carriages of the rich, and their freights of refined and elegant ladies, threaded their way among sections of the population so squalid and miserable that my heart ached at the sight of them'.

The squalor was even more astonishing to Continental visitors. As Taine described it in the 1860s:

> Every stairway swarms with children, five or six to a step, the eldest nursing the baby; their faces are pale, their hair whitish and tousled, the rags they wear are full of holes, they have neither shoes nor stockings and they are all vilely dirty. Their faces and limbs seemed to be encrusted with dust and soot. In one street alone there must have been about two hundred children sprawling or fighting.

It was in this restless city of contrasts that my grandfather was brought up, in a family struggling on the edge of poverty. He had been born in 1862, in Schull in County Cork, Ireland. His father James Sampson, a prosperous and cultured Cornish mining engineer, had married a formidable Irishwoman, Sarah Macdermott. James was much loved and well read: 'the most charming man I ever knew' recalled a cousin. But soon after John's birth James lost all his money when a bank in which he was a shareholder crashed with unlimited liability. He came to Liverpool in 1871 but fell ill and died the next year, leaving very little money and his widow to care for their 9-year-old son John and three other children.

Jack Sampson, as John called himself, was brought up by his strong-minded Irish mother as a Catholic and with a respect for books and learning. But at the age of 14 he had to leave school and was apprenticed for seven years to Alexander MacGregor, a lithographer and engraver in Liverpool. MacGregor was a demanding employer, initially paying Jack no wages and later only 10s 6d a week. His circumstances notwithstanding, Jack had already developed a passion for poetry and displayed a retentive mind for languages and grammar. While still an apprentice, and with a determination which amazed his friends, he taught himself at night-school and at home, absorbing a wide literature with scholarly accuracy. His three younger brothers were dominated by his personality and intelligence: his easy-going brother Jim later described how he never really understood 'that strange character that was my brother Jack ... his brilliant qualities and amazing powers of concentration and deduction that considered no labour too great to perfect everything he undertook to the very smallest detail'. And a family friend, James Crocket, recalled how 'Even then he was interested in gypsies and their language and I have a recollection of him reading poems in Romany between puffs of smoke.'

John Sampson stayed with MacGregor until he was 22, when his master retired, and then set up his own small business as a printer in the Liverpool Corn Exchange building, using an old hand-press so noisy that it drove the members of the Exchange out of the building. His first ambition – of which he was later cured by his friend Augustus John – was to be an artist and he acquired a broad knowledge of printing, typography and design, together with an elegant hand. But his real *métier* was philology, which he pursued with all the energy and passion for scholarship that marked the Victorian autodidacts. He was not much interested in money, spending all his spare time in learning about languages and phonetics. In the words of Scott Macfie, who was to become his close colleague in gypsy studies:

> It is difficult to conceive how a lad so fully occupied as he must have been, and in circumstances so strait, found time, means and energy to acquire by his own unaided efforts the scholarly attitude and the considerable scholarly equipment he later possessed, to become emphatically a very well-read man.

Sampson later told his wife how he had fortified himself:

> When I went to business – quite a small boy – among new people, I thought 'In future I will fight.' It was a very lonely time for me, dear, quite alone, no one to . . . advise me or help me to avoid the worst sort of mistakes: and now almost for the first time looking back at it I feel a little sorry for myself – sorry that my father, who loved me very much, had not been alive to help me. However, fight I did, for anything I wanted, which

chiefly was after all, only to be myself, to do what I wanted, to say what I thought, not to be crushed out or bullied down, to be able to follow what I thought right, chiefly to conquer what I thought was cowardice in myself, but which I now think perhaps may not have been.

He emerged from this experience with unusual self-discipline and confidence, having rejected any conventional religious faith, though he found some reassurance among Jewish friends:

I have always felt very grateful to the Jews, because, when I was young, and used to have hell and all its horrors thrust at me, and the ruin in this and every other world of the unbeliever, the occasional remembrance of this sane, talented and successful, and eminently religious people used to cheer my drooping spirits a little.

For anyone as interested as he in languages and speech, Liverpool in the late nineteenth century offered a ready-made laboratory of words. The cosmopolitan city was full of foreign enclaves and strange languages while the steam-ships and barques brought sailors' stories, rhymes and riddles from all over the world. His friend Glyn Davies remembered bringing Sampson a riddle he had picked up from the quayside: 'Roddle me riddle me rowlocks: wooden arse and leather bollocks.' Whenever they met thereafter Sampson would greet him with a shout of 'Roddle me riddle me rowlocks'. And though Sampson never left Britain, the world with all its riches came to him in Liverpool.

Philology provided rare opportunities for self-taught Victorian scholars from modest backgrounds, and through it men such as Henry Bradley, Joseph Wright and the phenomenal compiler of the *Oxford English Dictionary,* James Murray, were able to display their scholarship to academia. Murray's granddaughter and biographer later described how the great lexicographer achieved his breakthrough: 'In an age when paper qualifications, however useful, were not yet the essential passport to advancement which they have now become, perhaps in some ways the opportunities were greater than today.' Many of the philologists were amateurs, as the phonetician Henry Sweet complained in 1877: 'Most of us – indeed nearly all of us – are by force of circumstances compelled to work in a dilettante style. We cannot expect much from a philologist whose whole working day consists, perhaps, of an hour snatched from other labours.'

Philology was Sampson's passion, and the mysterious Romani language was to be his obsession. It began when at the age of 21 he first read the 'glowing romances' of George Borrow, who had died two years before in 1881. It was then, he wrote, that 'I first sought and cultivated the society of English Gypsies, collecting their language, folklore, and superstitions, and comparing them with their Continental kinsmen.'

The gypsies appeared all the more exotic as Western Europe became more industrialized and urbanized, and as their mysterious history was gradually unfolded. By then scholars had established, largely by studying their Romani language, that they had come from north-west India, and had migrated through Afghanistan, Persia and Turkey into Europe and North Africa (where they acquired the name Egyptians or gypsies). They had first been officially recorded in Greece and the Balkans in the early fourteenth century, but by the fifteenth century they were noted in most Western European countries, reaching Wales by the

1430s and Scotland by the end of the century. Everywhere they remained self-contained and distinctive, with their dark skins, their horses, tents and violins, and everywhere they practised the same trades, particularly as metal-workers, horse-dealers and fortune-tellers.

In each country the arrival of these strangers provided a test of local tolerance, as did later unfamiliar immigrants across Europe. In the late Middle Ages the gypsies succeeded in presenting themselves as penitents who were entitled to alms and succour from their Christian hosts, and some were protected with safe-conducts from local rulers, including a 'letter of protection' from the Holy Roman Emperor Sigismund to all his subjects. But by the mid-sixteenth century, with the coming of the Reformation, such hospitality had evaporated. Over the next two centuries the gypsies were oppressed and persecuted throughout Europe, accused of being vagabonds and thieves, and denounced as a corrupting influence. Each country devised its own laws and penalties, often ferocious. In Spain most gypsies were forced to settle in one place; many of those in Portugal were transported to Brazil; in Britain the laws were severe though increasingly ignored. But almost everywhere the gypsies defied their persecutors, retaining their unique lifestyle, living close to nature and maintaining their own traditions and strict family loyalties with extraordinary resilience and fertility.

By the late eighteenth century there were reckoned to be 700,000 gypsies in Europe. Yet while ordinary people still regarded them with fear, aristocrats, intellectuals and scholars came to be fascinated by them, particularly after they had traced their origins back to India. Romantic writers like Walter Scott and Goethe invested them with the splendour of the 'noble savage'. Their talents, particularly in music, came to be appreciated. In Hungary they had added their own rhythms to Magyar music to create a gypsy style which inspired sophisticated composers such as Liszt: a few virtuosi even married into the Hungarian aristocracy. In Russia gypsy orchestras became fashionable entertainers for grand families who respected their 'strong blood', while in Spain gypsies transformed Andalusian and Moorish dances and songs to create flamenco, a thrilling expression of all the gypsy defiance of decorum.

This wild allure was at odds with the relentless industrialization of the nineteenth century. The encroachments of factories and railways, with their strict timetables and disciplines, were fencing in the nomadic life of the gypsies. In many regions of Europe they were forced out of their traditional camping-places and made to settle in houses or shacks, though most managed to maintain their separate traditions and occupations, avoiding the wage-labour of factories or offices and adapting their old trades to other skills on the fringes of an industrial society, like knife-grinding or basket-making. As the century progressed censuses in Britain continued to record increases in the gypsy population living in tents, caravans or in the open air, reaching around 13,000 in 1891. Within big cities they established their own 'gypsyries', like Notting Dale in London, and near the cities they still found heaths and common land where they could haul caravans and pitch tents. Liverpool was full of such camping-grounds on the open heathland around the city.

Towards the end of the century eager British reformers began to try to regulate the gypsies, regarding them as a threat to settled industrial communities: they were led by George Smith of Coalville who from the 1870s pressed for gypsy homes to be inspected, and for their children to be assimilated into ordinary schools. Nonetheless, the majority of British gypsies, like those around Liverpool in the 1880s, were still part of an untamed, semi-rural world on the margins of an industrialized society. For most respectable British families the gypsies continued to represent a threat, whether to their moral values or their material possessions: they remained constantly suspected of thieving or cheating. But to writers of a romantic nature, to young rebels against bourgeois parents, or to adventurous philologists, the gypsy encampments became all the more alluring as the rest of the country became more suburban and conformist.

'The day is coming when there will be no more wild parrots nor wild wanderers, no wild nature, and certainly no Gypsies,' lamented the American philologist Charles Leland in 1882. 'Within a very few years in the city of Philadelphia, the English sparrow, the very cit and cad of birds, has driven from the gardens all the wild, beautiful feathered creatures whom, as a boy, I knew . . . So the people of self-conscious culture and the mart and factory are banishing the wilder sort . . .'

The gypsies had fascinated writers and poets ever since they arrived in Europe in the fifteenth century. Cervantes, who was said to have a gypsy aunt, described them as 'Lords of the Universe' whose palaces were tents. Shakespeare in *As You Like It* used the Romani phrase *ducdame* (*dukra me*: 'I foretell'). Most eighteenth-century writers saw gypsies as dangerous or dishonest: 'a vagabond and useless tribe' as the poet William Cowper described them. Jane Austen in *Emma* depicts Harriet being surrounded by a gang of gypsy children begging for money, until she is rescued by Frank Churchill. But from the late eighteenth century the Romantics were naturally fascinated by these mysterious outcasts. Sir Walter Scott portrayed the witch-like Meg Merrilies, singing to a wild tune in *Guy Mannering*. Shelley was captivated by encountering the 'children of nature': 'that little ragged fellow knows as much as the wisest philosopher', he told his friend Thomas Hogg. By the Victorian era gypsies were becoming an object of curiosity and compassion, particularly among those who rarely saw them. Queen Victoria herself was enchanted by meeting some on the Portsmouth road: 'they are such a nice set of Gypsies, so quiet, so affectionate to one another, so discreet, not at all forward or importunate, and *so* grateful; so unlike the gossiping, fortune-telling race-gypsies'.

The French Romantics had seen the gypsies in more erotic terms, as girl-dancers and singers with fatal attractions for young men. In *Notre Dame de Paris*, Victor Hugo had depicted a beautiful 17-year-old girl called Esmeralda who had arrived in France in 1482 having travelled through Hungary and Spain: innocent and passionate, 'with invisible wings on her feet', she lived 'in a whirlwind'.

The character of Carmen, the wayward gypsy seductress, had been created by Prosper Mérimée in his eponymous short story of 1845. Mérimée owed much to George Borrow from whom he borrowed many gypsy words; though he disputed Borrow's romantic view of chaste gypsy girls: 'most of the women are horribly ugly, which is one reason they're chaste'. Carmen was further popularized by Bizet's opera in 1875, while Verdi's *Il Trovatore* had in 1853 evoked their sinister life as outcasts of society. The word Bohemian, originally almost synonymous with gypsy, became associated with impecunious artists who defied bourgeois values – a milieu popularized in 1848 in a romance of student life in Paris by Henri Murger, *Scènes de la Vie de Bohème*, which in turn inspired Puccini's opera *La Bohème* in 1900.

The diaspora of the gypsies and their nomadic life extended their appeal. 'The only two races who have achieved true freedom are the Jews and the Gypsies,' Sampson claimed: 'The first because they have made every country their own, and the second because they can vacate any place as soon as it becomes wearisome to them.' In *The Zincali* Borrow wrote of their concern for money: 'Their leading passion is gain but only by fraudulent and insignificant means, for, in general, their minds are incapable of conceiving any great and extensive project.' Nor did he try to conceal their other faults: 'In no part of the world are they found engaged in the cultivation of the earth, or in the service of a regular master; but in all lands they are jockeys, or thieves, or cheats . . .' And in any capitalist society the true gypsies had an obvious difficulty in accumulating capital, for their belongings were burnt when they died.

Nevertheless, the Romanophiles liked to see them as belonging to the youth of the world, to the golden age of innocence. 'The Gypsy's faults then are mainly childish and natural,' wrote Eric Winstedt, a later enthusiast, 'and in this weary old world where childhood and all things natural are fast dying an unnatural death, is it not a pity to seek to transform nature's children?' Above all they defied the stifling conventions of a Victorian middle-class upbringing. In the words of the song:

> My mother said that I never should
> Play with the Gypsies in the wood . . .

Gypsies were portrayed in many legends, whether as the *femme fatale* who seduces the conventional young man or as the witch-like fortune-teller who foresees disaster. But romantic academics were particularly attracted to the legend of the Scholar Gypsy – the brilliant Oxford student who takes up with gypsies and forsakes his old friends and interests. The story was first published in 1661 by Joseph Glanvill who described how the gypsies 'could do wonders by the power of imagination'. It was revived nearly two centuries later in 1853 by Matthew Arnold in his poem 'The Scholar Gypsy'. John Sampson was naturally fascinated by it, for it brought together the scholar's pursuit of truth and the life of the vagabond:

> The story of the Oxford scholar poor,
> Of pregnant parts and quick inventive brain,
> Who, tired of knocking at preferment's door,
> One summer-morn forsook
> His friends, and went to learn the gipsy-lore,
> And roamed the world with that wild brotherhood,
> And came, as most men deemed, to little good,
> But came to Oxford and his friends no more.

3

The Wild Gypsy Dream

THE GREAT VICTORIAN traveller and writer George Borrow relived the role of the Scholar Gypsy in his own image of *The Romany Rye* – the title of his famous book, published in 1857. A rugged, strongly built man, he had travelled through much of England, Wales and Spain in the 1820s and '30s, recording his conversations with gypsies in their tents and caravans, and inspiring a younger generation of scholars and writers to look further into Romani culture. Borrow had an inexhaustible curiosity which did not confine itself to gypsies, and unlike many romantics he was not dismissive of industry. 'At Birmingham Station', he wrote in *Wild Wales*, 'I became a modern Englishman, enthusiastically proud of modern England's science and energy.' But he showed his real originality and influence in his escape from the industrial world, away to the open road and the 'wind on the heath'.

Many later readers found Borrow's muscular travels overburdened with long-winded dialogues and sometimes hard to believe: could he really have walked the 112 miles from Norwich to London in 27 hours? Philologists had to admit that he was an unreliable source. Sampson agreed that, though 'a great but careless linguist, Borrow was assuredly no philologist . . . While he has been the means of attracting others to the study of that interesting tongue, his own command of it was of the slightest.' In May 1888, at the age of 26 and while still working as a printer in the Corn Exchange building, Sampson wrote a scholarly letter to the publisher John Murray, explaining his own expertise in Romani acquired over several years, and providing a long list of errors and omissions in Borrow's *Romano Lavo Lil* which Murray was about to publish. Borrow for his part may not have minded young Sampson's judgement, for he despised 'a mere philologist; one of those beings who toil night and day in culling useless words for some magnum opus which Murray will never publish, and nobody ever read'. Writers and poets were naturally hostile to pedantic etymologists. As William Cowper described them in 1782:

> Philologists, who chase
> A panting syllable through time and space,
> Start it at home, and hunt it in the dark,
> To Gaul, to Greece, and into Noah's Ark.

But the language of the gypsies provided a special challenge because it helped to trace their past wanderings through its accretions and loan-words: as Alexandros Paspates explained: 'the true story of the Gypsy race is in the study of their language'. And it presented an extra challenge because it had been continuously preserved through speech, but not through the written word. The gypsy folk-tales, precisely repeated by story-tellers using traditional

words, provided a kind of substitute for a written literature, as in the days of Homer and the bards. To translate
the spoken word into a written alphabet was a major task
for the philologists, and a source of wonder to the gypsies
themselves; when Sampson was writing a letter for his
friend Kenza Boswell, Kenza exclaimed: 'Why, Rai, it looks
as easy when you do it as throwing turnips to a cow!'

Though critical of his errors and omissions, Sampson
remained under the spell of Borrow. As a fellow
Cornishman with Celtic blood he could identify with
Borrow's character and background, with the same
nomadic instinct, and with the same enduring romanticism. 'No more thrilling romance has ever been written',
he insisted much later, 'than Borrow's *Bible in Spain*.' He
was particularly fascinated by one passage in *The Romany
Rye* when Borrow talks with Jasper Petulengro and then
reflects:

I thought what strange people the Gypsies must have
been in the old time. They were sufficiently strange at
present, but they must have been far stranger of old;
they must have been a more peculiar people – their language must have been more perfect – and they must
have had a greater stock of strange secrets. I almost
wished that I had lived some two or three hundred years
ago, that I might have observed these people when they
were yet stranger than at present. I wondered whether
I could have introduced myself to their company at that
period . . . and then – and then – and a sigh rose from
the depth of my breast; for I began to think: 'Supposing
I had accomplished all this, what would have been the
profit of it; and in what would all this wild gypsy dream
have terminated?'

Beyond their philology, many of the gypsy enthusiasts were moved by quasi-religious feelings, as if these mysterious oriental tribes could take the place of the prophets of the Bible whose credibility was fading in a post-Darwinian age. My grandfather was part of a new generation who were scientifically minded but still longed for some escape from the rule of reason as they surveyed a bleak new world. 'To some peculiarly constituted people', he wrote, 'the name Gypsy is like that other great name that came as a hot blast from the East, maddening men's minds and constraining them to enroll themselves as followers.' The description echoes the words of the Catholic priest in *The Romany Rye*, who explains that the Popish system is really the same as the old Indian system: 'A hot blast came from the East, sounding Krishna; it absolutely maddened men's minds . . .' Sampson, who firmly rejected Christianity, would compare it to his own obsession with gypsies, as he explained later in a somewhat high-flown lecture:

> For we rate it as fair a thing to be a Romano Rai as others a poet or Christian. And I sometimes marvel, like the numismatist who collected Greek coins, that all the world is not for our pastime, though that indeed might spoil our sport. For whatever natural bent a man may have in his own mind, he may follow that the better by being a true Romano Rai, a Gypsy Scholar . . .

The gypsy enthusiasts inspired by Borrow longed to belong to a different world without material ambitions. Many of them, from Augustus John to Lady Eleanor Smith, liked to boast of gypsy blood. One biographer of Borrow later insisted (on doubtful evidence) that both Borrow's parents were partly gypsy. In fact it was Celtic more than gypsy blood which many had in common, but the real lure of the gypsies was in the mind rather than the blood. Gypsy enthusiasts were united by their longing for the open road, and escape.

Sampson was also inspired by Francis Hindes Groome, whose life came closest to that of the legendary Scholar Gypsy. The son of an archdeacon, born in 1851, he was set for a brilliant classical career until while at Oxford he became obsessed with gypsies and took off with them through England and Central Europe. He fell in love with the beautiful gypsy singer and dancer Esmeralda Lock, who was almost as captivating and volatile as her name-sake in Victor Hugo's novel. She was married to Hubert Smith, the town clerk of Bridgnorth, but Groome rashly persuaded her to go off with him. The lovers travelled through Europe, with Esmeralda singing and dancing in theatres, until in 1876 Groome settled in Edinburgh. There he helped to edit the new *Chambers' Encyclopaedia* for which he contributed the entry on gypsies for the 1888–92 edition, lamenting how 'the life-long tent-dweller in country lanes . . . is threatened with extinction'. But Esmeralda was no ordinary tent-dweller: she had become the archetypal wild gypsy singer, taken up by writers and painters including Dante Gabriel Rossetti, who is recorded as having painted her on the parapet of Notre Dame, like her predecessor in Hugo's novel. Esmeralda's comings and goings eventually drove the gentle Groome close to distraction until in 1898 he finally told her 'we must never meet on this side of the grave'.

It was Groome's book, *In Gypsy Tents*, published in 1880, which inspired John Sampson. The two began to correspond, and Groome lent his manuscripts to Sampson who in turn lent his collection of Romani stories. These helped Groome to compile his *Gypsy Folk Tales*, published in 1899,

Esmeralda

a debt for which he was deeply grateful: he compared the Rai to the brothers Grimm. 'Through these stories', he wrote, 'you should establish your name as *the* Folklorist of England and Wales.'

Groome appeared to outgrow his gypsy longings. 'Nothing in Groome's life is more remarkable', wrote David Patrick in the *Dictionary of National Biography*, 'than that he should have passed so swiftly from a veritable Bohemia of romance into the bondage of systematic labour . . .' But Groome's letters to Sampson reveal his agony over losing Esmeralda and 'the unprofiting exchange he had made in surrendering the call of the road, the ramble, the rustling woods for the bonds of the house-dweller, for the career of the scholar. The other was the only life that suited me, the only happy days I have known.' When Groome died at the age of 50 in 1902 Sampson lost a fellow-spirit, and wrote a poem in Romani, translated by Theodore Watts-Dunton, concluding:

> Scholar Gypsy, Brother, Student,
> Peacefully I kiss thy forehead,
> Quietly I depart and leave
> Thee whom I loved - 'Good night'.

But Esmeralda long outlived Groome, eventually settling down in North Wales, entertaining and corresponding with gypsy experts including Sampson, under her address: 'The Caravan, Prestatyn'.

Inspired by Groome and Borrow, in the 1880s Sampson embarked on his own pursuit of gypsies and their language. It was doubtless a welcome escape from the drudgery of the printing press. He would never forget the 'early enthusiasm', he wrote later, with which 'I would hail the thin smoke of a Gypsy wagon curling among the trees in some country lane, or the delight which I experienced when "drawing out" some venerable Gypsy'. He immersed himself in gypsy life, sometimes going native among them, and made close friends including Tom Lee, Lias and Eros Robinson, Florence Lovell, and Brucey and Mackenzie Boswell. Liverpool was a crossroads for many gypsy clans – Boswells, Lees, Locks, Lovells and Smiths – who camped on the open fields outside the city, at Walton, Greenlane, Tranmere, Sleeper's Hill or Wavertree Fields. There local families would meet up with visiting families from the rest of the country. In winter the gypsies would make occasional forays into Liverpool. In spring they would set off on their wanderings, some staying in the north-west to make money from gullible tourists at seaside resorts like Blackpool or Douglas on the Isle of Man, some travelling as far as Cornwall or the north of Scotland in search of business.

The Rai's obvious interest in gypsy words provided a passport into their world. Lias Robinson once broke a silence by saying 'Rai, here's a verse for you: it's for you, Rai:

> The Gypsy gentleman he comes here
>   To see the Gypsies,
> To hear the words they say,
>   And put them in his books.

'It is at least gratifying', the Rai commented, 'to find that, in frequenting my Gypsy friends' society, I am not credited with any baser motives than philological interest. On the whole, I felt rather flattered.' But his bond with his new friends extended far beyond philology. Lias Robinson's brother Eros remembered how young Sampson would join them in poaching expeditions in the early dawn, 'with big loose pockets in his jacket what would hold a rabbit or hare, wery conwenient like'.

Sampson also became fascinated by the bizarre characters among the gypsies and other inhabitants of the Liverpool underworld who spoke strange dialects, and he regaled his friend Scott Macfie with stories about them. There was the 'Flycatcher', for instance, who 'kept a common lodging-house and was loquacious in several cants'. There were the three evil-looking knife-grinders, Manni Connor, Double Devil and the Shah. There was 'Captain Kettle', the stammering taverner. There was the leather-jacketed Mr Spinetti, who turned the handle of an ancient, one-legged hurdy-gurdy faced with red silk. And there was William West, the Hercules of Birkenhead, who, after

killing a man, cheated the gallows only because a pros-
titute gave voluntary evidence that the fight had been
fair.

Between escapades he relished the complexities of the
gypsy vocabulary and grammar: 'I am a Sherlock Holmes
of thoughts, a detective of mental puzzles.' For two years
he collected vocabularies from the gypsies of Lancashire,
Yorkshire and Cheshire, tracing their links with oriental
words. As he later wrote to a friend:

> It is a beautiful thing to feel the *romance* of the words,
> to find in them a sort of diary of their wanderings, and
> as if one were wandering in a strange and exquisite
> museum, to notice in their ordinary speech here trea-
> sures carried from India, here scented and perfumed
> words from Persia, here Armenian antiquities, here
> strange loot stolen from wandering Kurds and Mongols,
> here again large stores raided from settled Greeks and
> Slavs, and a few odd trinkets annexed in Germany and
> France.

He could soon compete with established gypsy scholars,
with an accuracy which bordered on pedantry. 'I must
have had a German pedant as an ancestor,' he would later
tell his wife. German philologists had indeed brought a formidable rigour to the study of Romani. The first record of
the language was believed to be by an Englishman, Dr
Andrew Borde, who took down phrases from a conversation, probably with a barmaid, in 1542. But the first scientific study was by the German philologist Rüdiger who in
1777 discovered the link between Romani and the ancient
languages of India. A succession of German scholars followed, culminating in August Friedrich Pott who analysed
all the existing collections and established Romani as a sub-

ject for major scholarship. There was a comic irony about the despised and ragged gypsy people becoming the object of professional investigation, but the scholars' motivation was clear. As Scott Macfie described it:

> Romani has the antique beauty of a crumbling ruin, and presents the profoundly interesting spectacle of a language in various stages of decay, succumbing gradually to different forces – here overwhelmed by the infiltration of ancient words, there losing its own inflections and adopting the grammatical costume of its British, Spanish or Armenian hosts.

More ironically still, Romani was helped to survive by the treatment of the gypsies as outcasts and criminals, who guarded their language as a code undecipherable by police or magistrates. 'Thus they preserved Romani with sedulous care,' said Macfie, 'hid it as the greatest of their mysteries, and handed it down from mother to son until the present day with little alteration.'

Just at this time, in the late 1880s, two keen British scholars, William Ibbetson and David MacRitchie, conceived the idea of a Gypsy Lore Society as a kind of 'club of Romany Ryes'. They were joined as founders by Charles Leland, the American philologist, H. T. Crofton, the Lancashire historian, and the Archduke Josef of Austria, who had developed a paternalist interest in his gypsy subjects and had just published a gypsy grammar. 'Now there are five of us,' wrote Leland to MacRitchie, 'and a rum lot they are, as the Devil said when he looked over the ten Commandments.' The Society's first issue of its journal was published in July 1888 and it was this Society that gave a new focus to Sampson's gypsy studies. Soon he was included as one of the select club of Romany Ryes or Rais. His friends and colleagues came to call him simply 'the Rai'.

These Romany Ryes shared a fascination with the gypsy life and language but they also shared the limitations of paternalism and mutual admiration. As Sir Angus Fraser described them almost a century later, they had some attitudes which 'may set one's teeth on edge today . . . They fell over themselves to remind others that *they* were the first to make a particular discovery. They stressed how privileged *they* had been to be taken into the Gypsies' confidence.' Moreover they 'appeared to be uncompromisingly hostile to any adaptation that might draw the Gypsies closer to society'.

Sampson was interested in all kinds of underworld languages and 'cants' including rhyming slang, of which he kept a notebook:

Once a Week = Beak (magistrate)
Jumbo's Trunk = Drunk
Lancashire Lass = Glass
Pope of Rome = Home
God Forbids = Kids
Bees and Honey = Money
Finger and Thumb = Rum
Horse and Cart = Tart (girl)

However, it was not Romani that gave Sampson his first entry into academia, but a much more obscure language called Shelta that was used by the tinkers as a secret means of communication. Like Romani, it could be traced back to Shakespeare and beyond: 'I can drink with any tinker in his own language,' boasts Prince Hal in *Henry IV*. Shelta had first been discovered by Charles Leland whose researches into Romani took him on rough journeys through the countryside (he was once caught picking blackberries on the estate of Lord Tennyson, who teased him afterwards: 'I do believe you are a gypsy after all'). In the summer of 1876 Leland met a tramp on the road to Bath who, after exchanging a few words in Romani, confided to him: 'We are givin' Romanes up very fast – all of us is. It is a-gettin' to be too blown.' And he went on to explain that there was a new 'jib' which was 'most all old Irish, and they calls it Shelter'. Leland was excited by this discovery and sought out others who spoke the language. He spent the next two years verifying it, and in 1882 published his book *The Gypsies* which included a chapter on Shelta. But Leland remained baffled by its nature and origins: 'Shelta is perhaps the last Old British dialect as yet existing which has thus far remained undiscovered.'

When John Sampson came upon Leland's discovery he was at first sceptical of Shelta as an authentic language. 'It is a tribute to the secrecy with which Shelta has been kept', he wrote to Leland later, 'that though I knew Romani well, and at least five or six of the various cants of the road, I had never met with a word of Shelta except in the printed specimens given by you in *The Gypsies*. I often enquired about it in vain, and finally gave it up in semi-disbelief.' But Sampson was urged by David MacRitchie, then Secretary of the Gypsy Lore Society, to investigate it further. 'Probably he selected me as the least squeamish of his members,' he recalled. 'But even to me it sometimes occurred that Shelta was a language which no gentleman should be asked to collect.' He set about his task more scientifically than had Leland, using his greater experience of phonetics, Romani and the 'cant jargons', which enabled him to recognize true Shelta words. But his real advantage was his willingness to mix with very rough customers in the slums of Liverpool.

His first source was a knife-grinder in Liverpool called Brennan who later explained that he thought Sampson was 'an old lag who was making himself a bit wide'. Brennan seemed to be able to distinguish between Shelta and Romani and Cant, but he had only a limited vocabulary. Sampson then happened on two other knife-grinders as they were leaving their lodgings, together with an umbrella-faker with whom they worked in partnership.

These men were not encumbered by any prejudices in favour of personal decency or cleanliness, and the language used by them was, in every sense, corrupt. Etymologically it might be described as a Babylonish, model-lodging-house jargon, compounded of Shelta, 'flying cant', rhyming slang, and Romani. This they spoke with astonishing fluency, and apparent profit to themselves.

I worked for some time with these men, until I had collected all their words. Three more uncleanly and evil-looking men I never saw. One, an Irish tinker, passed under the name of 'Manni' Connor: another was known as the 'Re-Meather' or 'Double Devil': and the third was a tall cadaverous man called 'The Shah'.

My collections from these men were made in tinkers' taverns: and on the last occasion I was in their company we were seated in an inner room with wooden table and sanded floor. For obvious reasons I had placed them on the bench against the wall, occupying, myself, the other side of the table. Something, I forget what, aroused suspicion in their minds, and there was an air of immense trouble which I hoped at any rate would not be mine. I saw Manni rise to get between me and the door, while the Re-Meather was surreptitiously unbuckling his belt. Grasping the table with both hands, I turned it on its side, jamming them to the seat, the three blue and white pots of beer sliding down on them. Glancing back as I left the room, I saw those three worthies framed in a kind of triptych against the wall, and as I passed through the door I wished that I had more time to admire their astonished faces.

Sampson had to find other teachers, and he 'tracked Shelta from one squalid lodging-house and thieves' kitchen to another'. At last in the spring of 1890 a friendly knife-grinder (who was later jailed for being a fence) directed him to a 79-year-old tinker called John Barlow, who lived in an Irish slum of Liverpool, 'in a street which at the time was safe only for ... the dispensary doctor and the Catholic priest'. Barlow was a great discovery, 'a veritable tinker of the old order' who spoke Shelta which was unmixed with Irish, Romani or Cant. He told Sampson that Shelta-speakers were a caste more than a class, bound together both by heredity and by their trade as tinkers. He explained that the tinkers 'travel from place to place, in small bands or families, plying their craft, frequenting fairs, and trading in calves and asses; while their women gain money by hoaxing, telling fortunes, cutting cards, and tossing cups (divination by tea-leaves)'. Barlow insisted that the language was both very ancient and very secret, protected against divulgence to outsiders by great penalties. Writing to Leland, Sampson continued:

From him I collected a complete vocabulary, and from him, too, I obtained the words in their purest form and learned to distinguish Shelta from the other jargons mixed with it by the lower orders of grinders and hawkers. From him too I learned to believe in the antiquity of the language, and took down many little stories . . . I find it very common indeed on the roads, though ordinarily in a corrupt form and mixed with other cants. *All knife grinders speak it, more or less purely, but few of them know it by the name of Shelta . . . Irish horse-dealers speak it well. Borrow did not know it.*

Sampson was encouraged by Leland and MacRitchie to publish a paper on 'Tinkers and Their Talk' in the Journal of the Gypsy Lore Society in October 1890. 'Like all true citizens of the road,' he explained, 'the Tinkers protect themselves by the use of a secret language, variously known as Shelta, Sheldru, Sheldhru, Shildru, Shelter and ShelteroX, "Bog Latin", "Tinker's Cant", or "the ould thing".'

His paper was a remarkable achievement for a self-taught man of 28, and brought him into contact with Kuno Meyer, a lecturer at the University College of Liverpool who was an authority on the Celtic languages. At 32, Meyer was already a celebrated international philologist. Brought up in Hamburg, he had taught himself perfect English after spending two years as a boy in Edinburgh where he also acquired a passion for Gaelic. After taking his degree at Leipzig University he was appointed lecturer in Teutonic Studies at Liverpool at the age of 24, a position which provided him with the time and scope to pursue his Celtic studies in Ireland and Wales. With his black pointed beard and wide moustache Meyer soon became a university character, fascinating his colleagues with his witty mastery of English, Irish and Welsh, and befriending other aspiring philologists. He had already been studying the Shelta language, and was excited to see Sampson's article, which had been sent to him by Constable, the publisher. 'I have myself come across wandering tinkers on my tours through Ireland,' he wrote to Constable on 7 October 1890, 'but I never realised that their jargon could lay claim to such antiquity as is undoubtedly the case from Mr Sampson's evidence. This kind of Gaelic back-slang is at least as old as the eleventh century, for it is fully recognised and exemplified in Irish MSS of that period.'

Sampson soon took the opportunity to introduce himself to Meyer, as Scott Macfie later described:

> Kuno Meyer, hurrying home from a lecture, was followed by a tall, slender youth who after long hesitation plucked up courage to overtake and shyly accost the eminent Celtic professor. The modest young man was John Sampson, and they talked of Shelta . . . This meeting was a turning-point in Sampson's life, for Kuno Meyer, recognising his ability and the value of his work, gave him his friendship and introduced him to the brilliant circle that was planning to transform University College into the University of Liverpool.

Possessing the advantage of a deeper knowledge of Irish, Meyer took up the study of Shelta and Sampson introduced him to his previous source, Barlow, whom he repeatedly asked to see again. Meyer agreed that Shelta was a secret language of great antiquity and in his own paper paid a glowing tribute to Sampson who had 'succeeded in reading the riddle of Shelta, which had baffled all who approached it before him'. The joint achievement was hailed by other philologists including Leland who had first started the trail, and who added his own generous praise:

The result of the researches of these two philologists, Sampson and Meyer, was so strange as to seem absolutely romantic. For they firstly proved from intrinsic evidence that Shelta, of which they collected numerous specimens in the form of tales and songs, preserved many old Celtic forms or grammatical peculiarities which had disappeared from Old Irish, or Gaelic, or Welsh as now written. But beyond this, it was found by an Irish manuscript one thousand years old that the Celtic bards had an artificial secret tongue peculiar to themselves, known as Shelta, and of this, by extraordinary chance, a vocabulary had been written which still exists in the manuscript referred to. And the vocabulary made it clear beyond all doubt that this secret and sacred tongue of ancient days was identical with that of the British Tinkers of the present time.

Sampson continued to search Liverpool for Shelta words. Another future scholar and librarian, Glyn Davies, who was then working in the office of Rathbone's, the Liverpool shipowners, described how a tall stranger with a goatee beard came in to ask for his help with a list of Shelta words which might have Irish connections. Sampson took him to his home in Maryland Street to look through his card index where Davies spotted a few Irish words. Sampson also wrote an article on Shelta in the new edition of *Chambers' Encyclopaedia* and made plans to write a whole book about it with Leland and Meyer. Leland was indignant that other scholars did not take this ancient language seriously enough:

If it had been some infinitesimally trifling and worthless Himaritic or Himalayan up-country nigger dialect, every scholar in England would have heard of it long ago. But the old language of the bards – or at worst, an old Celtic tongue – is of no interest to anybody!

The book never materialized in Sampson's lifetime: it was left to a later scholar, Stewart MacAlister, to produce the definitive work, largely based on Sampson's notes after he died (and dedicated to his memory) though with a more cautious assessment of Shelta's antiquity.

In the meantime Sampson's printing business had failed in 1892. Never a good businessman, he now found himself at the age of 30 in the harsh surroundings of Liverpool with neither money nor job. Miraculously, however, through the mediation of Kuno Meyer, he was offered a position which suited him exactly – as first librarian of the University College of Liverpool.

It was an extraordinary invitation for a relatively unknown man who had left school at 14 with no formal qualifications in bibliography: unimaginable in today's universities. But the new university and its library were also starting almost from scratch. 'A small college, housed in an old asylum,' as Glyn Davies described it, 'possessed a library hardly adequate to the demands of a respectable night school.' The young Sampson already had a deeper scholarship than most of his colleagues: he was convinced that a librarian must be qualified and prepared to help university scholars. He soon proved his ability. At last his pedantry came into its own: he would personally catalogue all the books in the card-index for he agreed with William Blake that 'every minute particular is holy'.

It was a daunting task, and even more badly paid than most librarianships, the annual stipend being only £120. But the failed printer had found his golden opportunity. 'I began on a hopeless tack', he would tell my father, 'and only found my real vocation at thirty.' 'I felt myself in

Paradise,' he said later. 'It seemed to me a privilege for which the happy holder of the office should pay the Council generously, instead of being paid by the Council. Here one could live among books, not as a recluse in his study, but constantly meeting the most delightful people on the most delightful terms.'

The Rai

4

Academia and Bohemia

I̲T WAS A new and exciting experience to be an academic in the north of England at the end of the nineteenth century. In the wake of the Education Act of 1870, a succession of provincial colleges had sprung up as rivals to the ancient universities of Oxford and Cambridge. The new University College of Liverpool had only been established in 1882, ten years before Sampson joined it, and for its first twenty years it was not independent but affiliated, together with Leeds, Birmingham and Sheffield, to 'Victoria University' at Manchester. Rich Lancashire merchants had raised the necessary funds, led by the shipowner William Rathbone and including William Lever the soap king and Sir John Brunner the industrialist. The new college was set up in the slum district of Brownlow Hill, using the deserted lunatic asylum and culminating in a neo-Gothic tower rising above the grim terraces. But Rathbone insisted that 'living stones were more important than dead ones', and he dreaded the 'vulgar transatlantic megalomania

University College

which was preoccupied with grand buildings rather than professors' endowments'. For intellectual Liverpudlians University College marked the final emergence of Liverpool from its money-making, philistine past. As one of its early professors, Ramsay Muir, described it: 'In the midst of a community necessarily engrossed in the pursuit of gain, a fastness has been erected for the support and maintenance of the disinterested love of knowledge and of pure thought.'

The first principal of University College was Dr Rendall, a clever but conventional theologian – he worried when young women admitted as students played hockey in skirts ten inches above the ground. Though he gave the Rai a free hand in the library, the Rai thought him 'not very wise, strong or lovable' and complained that he treated his staff as a headmaster would. He had opposed the appointment of the brilliant Kuno Meyer and preferred 'little, local crawlers' who would be cheaper. In 1897, frustrated by the growing power of the university senate, Rendall resigned to become the headmaster of Charterhouse School, 'a post of less honour, greater ease and much greater emolument'.

The real moving spirit of University College was the Rathbone professor of history, John Macdonald Mackay, a bachelor who devoted all his time to the university, which he liked to compare with ancient Athens. He was a rugged Highlander and displayed a fiery eloquence and intensity. Mackay's lecturing style, recalled the professor of architecture Charles Reilly, seemed to be 'forever taking one to higher and higher planes of thought'. His lectures were however impeded by his habit of talking out of the window, so that many students preferred his smoother rival Ramsay Muir (later a Liberal MP), a preference which sharpened their bitter rivalry, since their fees were linked to the number of students they taught. Nonetheless, Mackay was the chief prophet of the new university, rallying a group of younger professors and lecturers who called themselves 'the New Testament' and who included Sampson, Kuno Meyer, Charles Reilly, Bernard Pares, Oliver Elton and Cecil Wyld. They were determined to extend the university's activities while maintaining academic freedom from commercial pressures. Mackay's missionary fervour is conveyed in a fine portrait by Augustus John and in a group portrait of the members of the New Testament by Albert Lipczinksi in which, with his right hand upheld, Mackay declaims to his audience. Both paintings still hang in the university.

Mackay's passionate zeal gave his colleagues a powerful sense of their mission. And though they were prone to provincial hyperbole and mutual admiration, their later records speak for themselves: they gave the fledgling college the self-respect it needed to compete with the ancient universities. Mackay saw it as a democratic alternative to the 'plutocratic monopoly of learning' which had dominated England for centuries. As he told teachers in Birmingham in 1888: 'There are whole streets of families, cloudy towns and scattered villages, for whom Oxford and Cambridge are little less remote than the House of Lords.' And he looked to the example of Germany to show how 'in countries where intellectual interest is keen, the universities are numerous and powerful'.

The college was almost ideally suited to the Rai's qualifications and ambitions. Not only was it a fast-growing centre of learning, but it had also already acquired a reputation in the subjects in which he specialized, philology and English literature.

The study of philology and phonetics made great strides in the late nineteenth century. In the 1870s young philologists like Alexander Ellis and James Murray, who was to become the editor of the grèat *Oxford English Dictionary*, had begun to study and record word-sounds throughout Britain. The excitement of their discoveries was reflected by George Bernard Shaw, who tried to produce his own phonetic alphabet and who was fascinated by the personality of the great phonetician Henry Sweet, his part-model for Professor Higgins in *Pygmalion*. The opening scene, in which Higgins records in his notebook the accent of Eliza Dolittle in order to trace which part of London she comes from, conveys all the thrill of the phonetician, the same thrill which Sampson felt when taking notes in gypsy camps. Henry Sweet – called 'Bitter Sweet' after his disappointed academic hopes – accepted a lectureship at Liverpool, but had to turn it down 'for private reasons'. Sweet recommended instead his friend H. C. Wyld, the etymologist author of *A Short History of English* who arrived in 1898 and became a close friend of Sampson's.

Philology was a cosmopolitan pursuit, with Germans in the lead, and Liverpool had already been influenced by the pioneering German linguist Vietor who left in 1884 for Marburg, where he became the chief rival to Sweet. In Liverpool Vietor had been succeeded by his fellow countryman Kuno Meyer who developed international interests while remaining a loyal German citizen, as his colleagues were later to discover. Kuno was determined to master the Irish language and literature which, as a young man, he had wanted 'to be the principal object of my life's work'. Celtic studies had attracted more foreign than Irish scholars and Kuno campaigned tirelessly for a summer school of Irish learning. This was eventually established in 1903, under the Irish philologist John Strachan, but Kuno remained committed to Liverpool and his university colleagues.

Sampson delighted in Kuno's exuberant scholarship and became a close friend. As he wrote on Kuno's fortieth birthday:

> Of all the swells in Univ. Coll.
> There's none so great as Kuno.
> He is the idol of his pals
> Though half his virtues few know.

Kuno wrote Sampson witty letters full of exotic references to Romani, Shelta and other languages and interspersed with occasional bawdy rhymes, and they both enjoyed experimenting with complex verse forms and scansions. For Kuno's fiftieth birthday the Rai wrote a poem in an obscure Irish metre which Kuno had said was unmanageable:

> Kuno Meyer
> Is a theme that might inspire
> Balder bards than I to worse
> Verse.

> Like a rock
> That has stood the tempest's shock,
> Kuno at this vain world's wiles
> Smiles.

The first chair to be endowed at Liverpool was that of English literature, a subject which, as Rathbone noted, 'was at that time practically untaught either at Oxford or Cambridge'. The professor was Walter Raleigh, a tall, thin-faced scholar, later professor at Oxford, the epitome of the 'Man of Letters'. He too became a lifelong friend of Sampson's, writing boyish letters and exchanging bold opinions, verses and jokes. He was also fascinated by

Sampson's adventures with both women and gypsies: Raleigh and his friends, noted a later university gossip, 'admired Bohemianism for the very reason that they were incapable of it themselves'.

Sampson conceived the notion of privately printing a very limited edition of Raleigh's minor verse, which became a very minor collectors' piece. The two men had complementary gifts. Sampson verged on the pedantic: 'literature is not my real *métier*,' he told Raleigh in February 1906, 'list-making is really what I love, list-making and analysing.' In contrast Raleigh, as Sampson later described him, 'could not tolerate the dry-as-dust notes of the ordinary text-book, or the pedantry of the scholiast. Literature meant more to him than language, and Life more than Literature.' Raleigh's only remembered work is his *Wishes of an Elderly Man*, which became one of my father's favourite poems:

> I wish I loved the Human Race;
> I wish I loved its silly face;
> I wish I liked the way it walks;
> I wish I liked the way it talks;
> And when I'm introduced to one
> I wish I thought *What Jolly Fun!*

Raleigh's cult of the littérateur is now very out of fashion; his book on style, which he dedicated to the Rai in 1897, was described by John Gross as 'one of the most stilted books ever written'. But his students found him inspiring. Stephen Potter, who was later to write *Lifemanship*, described how at Oxford 'We were silent before this ghostly tower, swiftly and quietly entering the classroom. His stride and his loftiness seemed always the result of a culture, never of a rank growth.'

Liverpool had academic stars in other firmaments, including the pioneering physicist Oliver Lodge who was then making historic experiments in radio-telegraphy – publishing a book in 1897 on *Signalling across Space Without Wires* – but who also held a lifelong belief in psychic phenomena and thought-transference. Sampson described him as

> an ether-intoxicated man, lost to mundane affairs in what seemed remote and obscurely shadowy investigations. Among my first memories of him is that of passing through the main hall in time to see the beginnings of wireless telegraphy, when a message, despatched from the old Physics building, was tapped off . . .

The Rai soon appeared in his element in this confident young university, able to continue his exotic researches while settling down into a secure job surrounded by congenial and original colleagues. And his new-found security was soon fortified, at least for a time, by falling in love.

In 1893, the year after finding his new job, Sampson met Margaret Sprunt, ten years younger than him. The Sprunts came from Forteviot in Perthshire, where Margaret's great-uncle James had been founder and editor of the *Perthshire Advertiser*. Margaret was a pretty and lively girl of 22 with her own sense of romance: one of the Rai's friends remembered her as 'a little girl of fourteen, with hair all flying about, and bubbling over with excitement always about things . . . Shelley or Keats or anything she had been reading just then'. She first met the Rai when her mother took her to the university library, and was swept up by his charm: 'never before had I met anyone', she told him afterwards, 'to whom I could talk so easily or with whom I was so much in sympathy'. He took her out boating at

Blackpool, and was soon determined to marry her. But her father David Sprunt took an early dislike to John Sampson, who was almost his opposite in temperament, and did his best to discourage his daughter from marrying this opinionated scholar with a 'microscopic income', who was so much older and who could so easily dominate her.

The Rai was a persistent and ardent wooer, writing seventy-seven love-letters in that year, full of the characteristic baby-language of the time, with endearments like kiddums or 'my chylde'. For the first time he appeared seriously smitten and he pinned his future on Margaret with an almost religious ardour: 'Dear, my dear,' he wrote on New Year's Eve, 1893, 'I find in reading your letters to me the kind of peace and comfort and consolation that a Christian finds in reading the Gospel.' At times his passion seemed almost to overwhelm him.

> Here at any rate is no man, standing outside himself and watching with interest and without danger, but instead a passion, that I want to guide me to happiness if I can but if not, a passion that must smash me up. For I have put all my hopes and ambitions in you. I remember how little casual sweethearts were ever a part of my life – episodes – how I used to long to feel something great enough to go for body and soul, seeking such a thing in religion and politics and never finding it, and now all the other things I care for sort of hang on to and belong to me only because of you.

For a girl of 22, such intensity must have been bewildering. Sampson, for his part, was worried about his own faults, as he revealed in his letters: 'Your goodness terrifies me, dear. Am I, can I be worthy of it?'; 'I wish often for your sake I were a more joyous or rollicking sort'; 'I can ask you not to quite dislike me when I am a sullen brute'; 'I fancy I am a nice person *not* to know'; 'Are you not ashamed of having such an IRISH husband?'; 'Would you explain to your friend that this bear does not dance, and has no social arts of any kind?' Yet he thought that he had genuinely been converted to a new kind of life: 'constancy never *used* to be my strong point, but *vous avez changé tout cela*'. And he insisted, somewhat prematurely as it turned out, that hypocrisy was the one vice that he lacked. He explained too that 'there was a time when I could live entirely by myself, when I needed no one much, nor cared much for anyone but could always stand clear away inside myself and see things go by. But now this is at an end.' He tried to share his literary enthusiasms, 'Have you seen the *Yellow Book*?', and recommended the works of Richard le Gallienne. And he encouraged her own verses which 'have a quaint simplicity and charm which reminds me of Blake, but you should give more attention to the laws of metre'.

Margaret's father, however, was obdurate: 'when I think of your father preventing it I get more and more angry silently in my soul'. So they were married in secret on 21 April 1894 at St Luke's Church by an archdeacon, without the knowledge of her father and with all the thrill of defiance. They also kept their marriage secret from the university for some time, and Margaret wore her ring concealed on a chain, until Kuno Meyer eventually broadcast it to the world, dismaying Mrs Rendall, the principal's wife. But Margaret's father still did not know in September, when he sent her off for three months to Valencia, presumably to forget about her impecunious lover. During her absence abroad the Rai's letters became still more passionate. In December 1894 he wrote a marathon missive in which the first pages are crossed out and surrounded by baby-language in capital letters: 'HIM

WAS A NASTY LITTLE BEAST, NEVER MIND HIM ZEN, HIM IS A PIG! HIM IS A BEETLE.' He was miserable without news of her:

> I walked about in the storm yesterday in a murderous destructive frame of mind – glad to meet no-one to quarrel with! . . . I daresay if one wants to be beloved that it is folly to love too much, for that brings all sorts of feelings up that can hardly make one a pleasant or companionable person.

He was soon transformed – 'Have just got your DIVINE LOVING letter' – and rejoiced:

> It is still rather a miracle to me how alike we feel and think without any effort to. This – the difference, total and absolute, of view between myself and the other 98 in 100 – has been with me all my life, and gives me the feeling of living among strangers in a foreign land . . .

The Rai and his wife were not really alike, and Margaret's identity often seemed overwhelmed by his dominating demands, as if she were no more than a receptacle for his imagination. She could not keep up with his restless adventures and was to remain trapped, like so many other wives, by her young family and by all the trappings of convention. Two years after his marriage, the Rai's first child Michael – my father – was born. He told his brother Walter in Canada: 'he is the most unceasingly active boy mentally and physically that I have ever seen'. That year, 1896, the family moved to Chatham Street, a once elegant Georgian terrace in Liverpool which had declined into a semi-slum. But the street was next to the university and was to house many academics; and there

Meg Sampson soon gave birth to another son, Amyas, and a daughter, Honor.

The Rai now appeared respectably settled in domesticity. But he soon embarked on a quite different romantic adventure which would change his life more fundamentally – without Margaret. In the summer of 1894, when she had just gone to Spain, he went camping in North Wales, whose wild splendours the railway had brought much closer to Liverpool. With his new university friends, among them Kuno Meyer, Walter Raleigh and Damer Harrison, he was in pursuit of gypsies. As one of them idealized it,

> exchanging for a while the flockbed of civilisation for the primitive couch of the earth, [we] went agypsying into Wales, and every evening pitched our tent now by a murmuring brook, now upon the shingle of the sea, then again among the heather on the mountain side, or in some woodland glade, where the hundred-throated chorus of birds awoke us at dawn, and the hooting owl startled us out of our slumbers at night.

In the middle of this Arcadian journey, as the Rai recalled,

> Kuno returned one evening to our camp-fire near Bala, bearing with him in triumph a captive Gypsy harper to enliven our little band with gallant Welsh melody, or with the gentle art of pennillion singing, of which he himself was a past master. Then for the first time I heard from a British-born *Kalo* the Romani language spoken not as an uncouth jargon, but as a pure Indian idiom, a veritable mother tongue, miraculously preserved from corruption by a single tribe among the hills and

fastnesses of Wales, which they had entered two hundred years before.

The harpist was called Edward Wood, a member of the Wood family who soon proved to be the custodians of this pure Romani language. Edward was then 46: as Scott Macfie described him six years later, 'A Jewish-looking little man with hook-nose, hanging lower lip and a moustache'. He played the Welsh triple harp, and had been a domestic musician for the Cornwallis-West family at Ruthin Castle. He had married successively two daughters of another gypsy harpist, John Roberts. He did not speak Romani at home, but he told the Rai: 'I was so used to hearing my father talk Gypsy when I was young, that I can never forget it.' He had a good memory, and was careful to distinguish between real and spurious gypsy words. 'If I knew that word', he would tell the Rai, 'I would have it stuffed.'

The Rai realized that 'the ancient Romani tongue, so long extinct in England and Scotland, had been miraculously preserved by the Gypsies of the Principality'. To a philologist it was a treasure trove, 'like finding a tribe of organ-grinders who among themselves spoke Ciceronian Latin'. He remembered how George Borrow had dreamt of living among the gypsies when their language had still been pure: 'I thought what strange people the Gypsies must have been in the old time . . . in what would all this wild gypsy dream have terminated?' Yet Borrow, when he walked through 'Wild Wales' in 1854, was unaware of this gypsy tribe; and, as the Rai listened to Edward Wood talking casually in this ancient language, 'I felt almost with a sense of awe that Borrow's dream was fulfilled in my own person, and that this was the very speech of two hundred years ago.'

Edward Wood now became the Rai's mentor and guide to this magical language, as he later recollected:

from this gentle and very intelligent friend, himself trilingual like all the members of his family, I learned to master the new sounds, words, and inflections. From Edward, too, I ascertained the habitat and favoured camping-places of the scattered scions of the *'teulu Abram Wd'*, with their congeners the Griffithses, Robertses and Prices, and as the result of many pilgrimages throughout North and Central Wales became acquainted with almost every Welsh Gypsy of the original stock.

For the next year the Rai spent as much time as he could with the harpist, who was his sole instructor in deep Romani. He first had to discard the language that he had learnt from other gypsies and to 'begin all over again like the merest tyro'. It was very hard work, as he told Margaret:

He does know the language splendidly, but hang it! he is so silent you can't get anything out of him without tremendous exertion. Have to do his thinking and your own too. I am a merciless person when I am on the collecting lay. I feel what a hardship it is for the poor things to have to grind their rusty memories and unused machinery of their minds for me, but I keep them at it. I wonder if they hate me. Not that I think that Wood does . . . I got some beautiful things from him today. Ablatives or adverbs and queer things of that sort.

And he added, 'Somehow they don't at all console me for the want of you. Man does not live by philology alone.' But it was an all-engrossing pursuit. Sometimes Edward would come to Liverpool and play at The Welsh Harp, an old-fashioned pub by the docks, with wooden tables and wooden benches, where the Rai would sit with his friends.

In a corner of the room propped up on tall cushions sat the Harper, who rolled his head round in a rather ghastly way, while all around sat all sorts of sailors, Eisteddfodd singers, and Welshmen generally. Some of them sang quite well, and I should not fail to tell you how it impressed me, the marvellously grand sounds of the language, the words ending in *od*, the emotion of the singers and hearers and especially of the sailors, some of whom were splendid fellows.

Two years after this first breakthrough, the Rai discovered a cousin of Edward's who proved still more valuable. In the summer of 1896 the harpist Lloyd Roberts, another child of John Roberts, led him to the banks of the lake Tal-y-llyn, on the slopes of Cader Idris – still today a desolate spot with its grey slate expanse, though only a few miles inland from Barmouth Bay. There he took the Rai to the log cabin of Matthew Wood and his four boys, Harry, Manfri, Howell and Jim. When Lloyd Roberts shouted for Matthew, he came out of his cabin, an energetic woodcutter of about fifty, with glossy black ringlets reaching to his shoulders. The family were all faithful conservers of the pure Romani language and raconteurs of ancient folk-tales, and they welcomed the Rai as someone who spoke Romani as deep as their own.

Soon afterwards they moved to Abergynolwyn, a tiny village three miles from the lake, in the heart of the countryside which they most liked because of its rivers and wildness.

In July the Rai followed them there, staying at the Railway Hotel, which remains today the only inn in the village, near the miniature railway line which now serves tourists coming up from the coast at Towyn.

'Observe the aristocratic address', he wrote to Margaret:

This is a lovely little village with steep green hills immediately before my window – a small village green with a huge pile of timber on it – the trees in fact which Mat Wood cleared off the slopes at Tal y Llyn when I was there before. My old host looked in here today – so surprised when he saw me.

I have done a lot of work already – another good tale, many grammatical examples and yesterday at Wood's house I took down a number of queer little 'sense riddles' which will be a pretty novelty in a grammar. Here is a rather nice one:

Four white ladies chasing each other yet they never catch each other.
Answer: Windmill.

The Rai later described an exotic evening with his teacher:

Matthew, for my delectation, has produced an old fiddle, and, with true Gypsy ingenuity, has improvised a bow from an ash plant and hairs plucked from the tail of a cart horse. In this *Wolsitika t'em* every one sings, every one loves music, and music is a pass-key to brotherhood. Most evenings see a merry gathering in the little *kirčuma*, and more than one have we prolonged into the small hours of the morning, sitting in the old tiled kitchen from whose low beams hang fragrant herbs, strings of onions, and smoke-dried hams.

Sampson was to spend many such university vacations with Matthew Wood at Abergynolwyn, recording both words and folk-tales 'in a sort of frenzy,' as he told his old friend Francis Hindes Groome. 'No work could be more exhausting. To note every accent, to follow the story, and to keep the wandering wits of my Romani raconteur to the point, all made the work trying.' And to Charles Leland he wrote: 'at times I have spent weeks without hearing English spoken, for the natives speak Welsh, and the Gypsies invariably Romani'.

But Matthew Wood was a shy and reserved man – his family called him 'the mole' – possessed of a gypsy restlessness. One day, having cleared the hillside of trees, he walked away and disappeared without trace for nine years.

In the meantime the Wood family transformed the Rai's career: for he was now determined to spend all his spare time compiling a great dictionary of this pure Romani language, which would trace its connections with Sanskrit, Persian and the European languages. He was not to know that it would take thirty years to complete.

Yet another distraction from domestic life appeared in the shape of Augustus John, who arrived in Liverpool in the spring of 1901, when the Rai was 39, to teach at the art school affiliated to University College. John was a dashing young artist of 23 with an auburn beard, earrings and exotic clothes who had already fascinated or horrified the university staff. In the Rai – though almost twice his age – John quickly found a lifelong friend, as he describes in his autobiography *Chiaroscuro*:

> This meeting turned out be one of the outstanding events of my life. John Sampson, upon his introduction to a young long-haired stranger bearing all the stigmata

of a *Romantic*, roused himself at once (for he too was a romantic in disguise). Discarding what I learnt later to be his usual protective colouring in society, compounded of a certain aloofness and disdain, while retaining a magisterial style combined with a rare and sometimes sardonic humour, he at once captured my sympathies. In a word, I was enchanted . . .

He introduced me to his Gypsy friends, and we made a practice of visiting the tents together. Under his tutelage and by personal contact with the Gypsies, I soon picked up the English dialect of Romani . . .

John Sampson could turn a phrase better than most. If his manner and speech verged on the ponderous, it was only in keeping with his physique, which was big and portly . . .

Sampson's measured utterance, overbearing manner and sardonic humour, which he was apt to accentuate with strangers, served him as a conversational style well calculated to reduce his interlocutor to the condition of discomfort aimed at, while protecting his own highly vulnerable sensitivity from attack. It used to move me to irrepressible merriment.

John was fascinated by 'the majestic Sampson', as he described him to their mutual friend Mary Dowdall, 'the large and rolling Rai – he reminds me of a magnificent ship on a swelling sea'. Or as he later depicted him in his autobiography: 'he made an imposing figure as he strode along, with his battered hat at a commanding angle, his cutty alight, his chin thrust out, and his powerful legs moving rhythmically'.

The Rai in turn romanticized John, even writing a rather embarrassing poem in Romani called 'The Apotheosis of Augustus John', which he translated into English, depicting the Lord as appointing John as his Grand Vizier. 'Bid him bring with him his special friends,' he tells St Peter, 'and some pretty girls, and a band of Gypsies, men and women, and a few Romany Ryes.' John's biographer, Michael Holroyd, regrets the Rai's influence over him: 'Altogether, Sampson encouraged the stage Gypsy in John, and helped to promote an image of larger-than-life, amorous, wine-bibbing jollity little to the taste of post-Georgian connoisseurs.' The Rai in fact was never a publicist, and John hardly needed encouragement. But Sampson was certainly fascinated by the artist's panache and genius, while John's reciprocal admiration and generosity disarmed any jealousy. As the Rai later wrote to my father:

> John has certainly been favoured by the gods. Strong, handsome, a genius, beloved by many men and women, with a calling which is also his chief pleasure and allows him the most entire freedom, successful beyond his dreams or needs and assured of immortality as long as art lasts. It is almost more than one mortal deserves, but somehow it seems all right in his case.

The two men were united by their obsession with gypsies and together explored their camping grounds outside Liverpool, particularly an expanse of waste ground called 'Cabbage Hall', where many well-known gypsy families, led by the Boswells, spent the winter months. John described how

> Under Sampson's aegis I was made welcome in the tents and got to know their occupants, who bore such exotic names as Noah, Kenza, Eros, Bohemia, Sinfai, Athaliah, Counseletta, Alabaina, Tihanna, Simpronius,

Saiforella ... By showing a sympathetic interest in their speech and customs, and without neglecting the lubricative medium of liquor, the collusion of the men was assured: they admitted us into their confidence and disclosed their tribal secrets unreservedly. The Chais, or young women, were more difficult: provocative and yet aloof, they were capable of leading the tyro into a region of pitfalls, where indiscretion might land him in serious difficulties. By the exercise of an oblique and derisory intelligence, Gypsy girls are eminently qualified to take their own part.

This fascination with gypsies distinguished John from most of his artistic predecessors and contemporaries. For as Eric Rowan notes in his study of painters in North Wales:

The previous, *fin de siècle* generation of artists – exemplified by Aubrey Beardsley, Wilde and Whistler – had been men of the city, equally at home in London or Paris, and content to experience nature through the windows of a railway carriage. John and his fellow-enthusiasts inherited these metropolitan tastes but inverted the attitude to nature. Unlike the Parisian bohemians, confined to cafés, boulevards and garrets, they admired the true bohemians who were unburdened by material cares, who were footloose, nomadic, untrammelled and free to travel the open roads in painted caravans – or so it seemed. To put it into literary terms, it was the triumph of Borrow over Murger. But while most other devotees of the gypsy cult were content to rhapsodise about it in the comfort of London drawing rooms, John put admiration into practice and took to the open road with his two women and numerous children packed into a

Ida by Augustus John, c. 1902

couple of caravans . . . He acquired a lasting admiration
for 'the travelling people' and a deep interest in 'the
affairs of Egypt', since their romantic, nomadic life
appealed to some basic frustration in his nature.

In Liverpool, John's young wife Ida – who produced
their first baby David in January 1902 – enjoyed the

company of both the Rai and his wife, and she later became Margaret's close friend and confidante. The two lonely young wives with their dominating, philandering husbands took solace in each other's concerns, exchanging notes about babies and domestic worries, and writing with charming directness. And though each was sadly maltreated and neglected, they remained loyal.

The Johns stayed briefly with the Sampsons in September 1901, Ida telling her mother that they were 'delightful people': later they lived only three doors away, at 138 Chatham Street. Ida was fascinated by the 'huge and charming' Rai: 'Sampson came in last night and we talked till half past 12,' she wrote to her father. 'He sits and says things in a heavy sort of way.' And when Ida gave birth to David, the Rai wrote a verse in Romani (the sentiment of which he was later to echo in a letter to my mother):

When I heard thou hadst become a Mother, I said to myself that thou must indeed be a talented young woman.
I myself labour year after year to create a book or add to learning; but how little do I see for all my pains . . .

The two men kept up a jocular correspondence, much of it in Romani. John often wrote with an artist's brush in huge letters and the Rai sometimes reciprocated with his own big letters, signing off with the gypsy symbol of a reversed swastika. John was always affectionate but impatient about the Rai's hypochondria: 'Don't talk of snuffing out just yet. You've evidently got indigestion.'

The Rai sent poems or gypsy songs and stories to John, who in turn sent sketches of gypsies and others. 'Now

Sketch of the Rai by Augustus John

partner, you must play straight. No publishing songs without my collaboration – that is the bond,' John wrote from Essex in 1905, trying at the same time to persuade the Rai to come south. 'There are also some German Gypsies in London – so two Romany Rais would find plenty to do just now in town.' When the Rai translated some verses of Fitzgerald's *Rubáiyát of Omar Khayyám* into Romani, John drew a sketch of a gypsy boy and girl as a frontispiece, a generous gesture he would often repeat. John also made at least two vigorous sketches of the Rai which capture his romantic eye: one of them (which I later inherited) was exhibited at the New English Art Club and has been much reproduced.

John enjoyed making fun of the Rai's eccentricities. 'He

is more of an old maniac than ever,' he told his mistress Dorelia in 1909, when he was revisiting Liverpool. 'The Rai is in an awful state,' he wrote again soon afterwards: 'He has five white hairs over his brow which wiggle mysteriously.' Sometimes he would tire of the Rai's dominating presence:

> Sampson's visit to London lasted rather too long; growing tired of his company, I abandoned him in the Euston Road while he was immobilized under the hands of a shoe-black. I made my way to Matching Green, Essex, where I was then living. By a curious hallucination I seemed to hear the Rai's voice croaking in my ear all the way. Like making a new friend, to break with an old one, even at some physical discomfort, may be a refreshing experience. Doubtless Sampson's relief was as great as mine.

But the two men always patched up their quarrels, and the Rai would continue to trust and admire John, and to confide his secrets – or most of them.

In Liverpool the pursuit of gypsies provided a rebellious cause for a group of intellectual rebels, led by the Rai and John, against the constraints of bourgeois convention. The most aristocratic among them was Mary Borthwick, the spirited younger daughter of Lord Borthwick. She had married an ambitious young Liverpool lawyer, Harold Challoner Dowdall, who became Lord Mayor of Liverpool in 1908. Mary persuaded her husband to have his mayoral portrait painted by Augustus John, who produced a flamboyant half-comic masterpiece with the tall Dowdall as a kind of Don Quixote standing beside his clerk as Sancho Panza. (The painting appalled Liverpool's own Walker Art Gallery and now hangs in Melbourne.)

Dowdall himself was a conventional barrister who soon became a judge, but Augustus found Mary 'the most engaging character in Liverpool'. The Rai also loved her sense of fun and called her the Rani, or Lady; while she wrote to him as 'my dearest Rai' and signed herself 'always your devoted Rani'. The Rai recalled one evening when he was dining with his friends at the chief hotel in Llanrwst in North Wales. The Rani startled the other guests 'by threading her way among them with fairly kerchiefed head, short striped petticoat, bare legs and sandals, carrying aloft a capacious blue and white jug of beer for the delectation of our party.'

The Rai also discovered a romantic Irish girl whom he called Doonie and whom he soon introduced to Augustus: the Rai wrote verses to her and John did some vivid drawings, though neither have been traced. Later a handsome, black-bearded Polish painter called Albert Lipczinski arrived in Liverpool knowing no English but with an introduction to Augustus who in turn introduced him to Doonie. She spoke Polish and served as his interpreter; and soon afterwards they married.

Three years after John's arrival another rebellious newcomer came to Liverpool. Charles Reilly was the new professor of the School of Architecture who succeeded the pedestrian Fred Simpson. Reilly later became an influential architect and consultant to the most daring English building of the 1920s, the glass-fronted store of Peter Jones in Sloane Square; but in 1904 he was unknown. Reilly cut a theatrical figure in the streets of Liverpool with his wide-brimmed black hat, black cloak and silver-knobbed ebony walking stick. The Rai quickly approved: 'Charles Reilly is a white man not a bloody mulatto like Simp,' he wrote to Augustus, 'And married to a nice girl of 19.' Reilly had his own

'Doonie' by her husband Albert Lipczinski

Bohemian tendency – he later maintained a *ménage à trois* with Doonie and his wife – and he delighted in the rebellious spirits who escaped from bourgeois Liverpool to the wilds of North Wales:

Liverpool in 1904 was still arguing about a caravan on its way there going down Bold Street at the fashionable hour with the Hon. Mrs Dowdall, her one aristocrat, seated stockingless – a first-class event in those days – on the steps and behind her the Sampson and John families, with Dowdall, a rising young barrister now the County Court Judge, and John riding on nags behind.

Reilly was impressed by the inhabitants of the new university, and particularly by those of the 'semi-slum' Chatham Street where he was to live himself and which housed the Rai, Augustus John and also the young composer Eugene Goossens, later a world-famous conductor. In that one street, Reilly wrote in his own memoir, 'were three men to whom it would not be too much to apply the word "genius". The Corporation should note the numbers of the houses where they dwelt.' But he was most interested in the Rai:

Sampson was big and monumental, clad generally in a velvet jacket, with a strangely gentle voice and an insight into character of friend and foe almost as keen as Mackay's. There was something extraordinarily lovable about him in spite of his likeness in manner and vast knowledge to Dr Johnson.

These young academics could openly pursue their romance with the gypsies beyond the confines of the city. But there were strict limits to the defiance of academic respectability. And the Rai was becoming increasingly divided between the two sides of his life, his respectable family ménage soon being threatened by his obsession with the gypsies and the lure of Bohemia.

5

Grammar and Girls

IN THE EARLY twentieth century many English writers and intellectuals were bent on escaping from the surrounding materialism and squalor of an industrial world. Horrified by the results of the huge growth in population – mass production, the popular newspapers, the advertising hoardings, and the endless rows of identical houses in the suburbs or along the coastline – they hankered after a pre-industrial world. They looked back to folk-tales, to country dances, to nostalgic poetry such as A. E. Housman's *A Shropshire Lad*, and searched for unspoilt communities and 'natural aristocrats' – whether in tribes in other continents, or among the Scots, the Welsh or the Irish. English scholars and writers began to re-evaluate their own literary heritage, returning to more mystic writers and poets. And in William Blake, as the imaginative rebel against conventional Christianity and materialism, they found a particular champion. Blake had largely been ignored by the Victorians and was not included in William

Palgrave's *Golden Treasury of Verse* compiled in 1861. But, rediscovered by Swinburne in 1868, he began to enjoy a major revival in the early twentieth century.

In Liverpool, the Rai found in Blake the same feeling of liberation and magic that he had discovered amongst the gypsies. He had loved Blake's poems as a child, and enjoyed parodying his lyrics, sharing his enthusiasm with Walter Raleigh who relished 'Billy' Blake as a rebel against society: 'It would be difficult', Raleigh wrote, 'to find anywhere a more complete and eloquent statement of the creed of Anarchy.' From Oxford, Professor Frederick York Powell recommended in 1901 that Sampson edit a small book of Blake's lyrical poems for the Clarendon Press, to which he agreed 'in a somewhat light-hearted mood'. But after comparing the texts the Rai despaired of a reliable version and proposed instead that a full critical edition be prepared before the small volume. With immense energy he set about collating all the engravings and manuscripts containing Blake's poems, much helped by two young women in his bibliography class, Eileen Lyster and Dora Yates.

In 1903 he began a long and detailed correspondence with the American collector W. A. White in New York who owned the precious Rossetti Manuscript of Blake's lyrics. Raleigh, who also corresponded with 'old White the millionaire', complained that a letter from him 'smelt, not of money, but of the suspicious habits engendered by money'; and the Rai agreed. White nevertheless provided him with exact transcripts of the poems and answered his detailed questions meticulously. When in June 1905 the collector bought a mass of other Blake originals which had belonged to Frederick Locker-Lampson, the Rai was excited to discover among them the long-lost Pickering Manuscript which provided new rectifications of Blake poems.

The Rai's edition of Blake's poems was published by

Oxford the next year as was his smaller selection. He did not expect many people to buy the full edition: as he told Raleigh in November 1905,

> It only saw the light, to die,
> Did Mr Sampson's screed,
> A book whom there were none to buy,
> And very few to read.

Nevertheless, the two books were soon accepted as the definitive text and encouraged a new wave of interest in Blake. The poet Arthur Symons was moved to write his own book on Blake two years later, with much help from the Rai. And the Rai with Oliver Elton persuaded two young Liverpool scholars, D. J. Sloss and J. P. R. Wallis, to begin editing Blake's prophetic writings, which they completed twenty years later when they explained that 'If our text has merit, the credit lies largely with Dr Sampson.'

The Rai's edition of Blake's lyrics established his scholarly reputation. In the words of Lytton Strachey's review:

> Mr Sampson's minute and ungrudging care, his high critical acumen, and the skill with which he has brought his wide knowledge of the subject to bear upon the difficulties of the text, combine to make his edition a noble and splendid monument of English scholarship.

The rarefied lifestyle of Strachey and his Bloomsbury friends was a world away from the earthy escapades of the Rai or Augustus John. 'When I think of him,' Lytton Strachey wrote about John to Duncan Grant, 'I often feel that the only thing to do is to chuck up everything and make a dash for some such safe secluded office-stool as is pressed

by dear Maynard [Keynes]'s happy bottom.' But Bloomsbury respected scholarship. Geoffrey Keynes, a surgeon
and bibliophile and the younger brother of the economist,
had been enchanted by Blake after seeing his engravings in
a Cambridge bookshop and began to prepare a bibliography of the poet's works. In 1910 he submitted it to the Rai,
who he knew was 'reputed to be a somewhat formidable
personality', and went to see him in Liverpool.

> I found him in his Library embodying the authentic pres-
> ence of a Dickensian savant and Man of Letters. Some-
> what obscured by a cloud of tobacco smoke, he sat, a
> heavy figure with a florid countenance, hunched in an
> armchair at a great desk covered with papers, a gold-
> rimmed pince-nez dripping off his nose over a wide
> waistcoat scattered with portions of food that had not
> reached his mouth, but with a kindly grey eye.

The Rai left Keynes in no doubt about his view of the
bibliography: 'I take it', he wrote, 'that in its present form
it is merely the roughest of rough drafts and would be con-
siderably rewritten and rearranged before being offered to
the public. In my opinion no time or trouble should be
grudged to make the book a perfect specimen of its kind.'
And he followed with practical suggestions for improving
it. Keynes immediately began rewriting the whole bibliography on a different plan, and a year later submitted it to
the Cambridge University Press. They sent it on to the Rai
in Liverpool, who promptly wrote a still more withering
report.

> Only in a strangely limited sense can the work be
> described as a Bibliography of William Blake ...
> Mr Keynes's descriptions of books show throughout a

lack of familiarity with the methods of exact bibliography . . . In many cases Mr Keynes seems to have taken his facts from other bibliographers, obviating the necessity of acknowledgement by restating them in his own fashion, though not always, perhaps, more lucidly and sometimes with positive misunderstanding.

Once again Keynes humbly accepted the criticisms, and again rewrote the whole book, taking three years and adding an exhaustive section on the illuminated books. At last the Rai was 'distinctly respectful': Keynes found his report was now 'couched in almost flattering terms' and the bibliography was eventually published by the Grolier Club in New York. The Rai was glad, he wrote afterwards, that his criticisms 'did not – to borrow a feline figure – get your back up . . . I have got to feel that the only way in which an opinion can be helpful is just to blurt it out, and let it go at that.' Keynes continued a very friendly correspondence with the Rai, whose characteristic signature 'came to mean so much to me'. And when he eventually published his own edition of Blake, he generously acknowledged the pioneering work of the Rai who 'set an example of accurate scholarship which might never afterwards be disregarded'.

The Rai was now a recognized 'man of letters', with his own unassailable expertise on Romani and Blake, and he was meeting and corresponding with literary lions with confidence. When he met George Saintsbury, the omniscient professor of English at Edinburgh, he was most struck by 'his wonderfully coloured mulberry nose. I then thought it a misfortune only, and it never occurred to me to connect it with the possession of a cellar.' He also met W. B. Yeats (whose earlier edition of William Blake, he complained, 'did not much respect the integrity of Blake's text') and liked him, 'though he is a little affected, and professes to believe in fairies'.

Another of the Rai's regular correspondents was Theodore Watts-Dunton, Swinburne's companion, who had written a bad novel about gypsies called *Aylwin*; but he was dismissive of his talents. 'Can you think of anything laudatory that might be said of the old man's brand of poetry?' he asked Walter Raleigh in February 1906 after having been invited to review Watts-Dunton's poems: 'If so tell me for I cannot.' Years later he discussed him with Robert Bridges, the poet-laureate: 'He had referred to himself as a humbug, and I was content to leave it at that.' Bridges replied by quoting some caustic verses he had written after Watts-Dunton's death, beginning:

> He lives in other people's ways
> In hope to get a shove,
> A man whom it was wise to praise
> And difficult to love . . .

In May 1909, aged 47, the Rai was given remarkable recognition for a man who had left school at 14: an honorary doctorate of letters at Oxford. 'Romany and Shelta', the Rai was assured by Eric Winstedt, 'and not Blake were the passwords that opened the rock.' His chief backers were Walter Raleigh and Herbert Greene, the President of Magdalen, who were both members of the Gypsy Lore Society, while Donald MacAlister, the principal of Glasgow University who was also a member, added his support. It was a heady experience. The Rai stayed at Magdalen, and after receiving his degree and being flattered in Latin by Gilbert Murray he was given a dinner with Romani names for each course on the menu, beginning with *Matcho* (Salmon) and ending with *Shutlo Kova* (Caviar). On the facing page of the menu was printed a Romani translation of 'A book of verses underneath the bough'. In his after-dinner speech President Greene (a voluble Irishman) ventured to add a political dimension to the pursuit of gypsies: 'When progress and reform involve – unavoidably it may be – the gradual disappearance of an ancient race, and the loss of their old-world language and traditions, then I am sure that the feeling of regret that this must be so, will be shared, at least here in Oxford, by the reforming Radical and the unregenerate Reactionary.'

Liverpool saw the degree as a tribute to the university and to Romani studies as much as to the Rai himself: the open road of the gypsies could also be the road to scholarship. But the Rai welcomed a change of status: he kept his doctor's robes in a special tin box. He was now not just the Librarian but also the Doctor.

It was the gypsies, much more than William Blake, who satisfied the Rai's romantic yearning and rebellious instincts, and he was relieved when he could be finished with Blake's obscurities. As he told Raleigh in February 1906:

> I didn't *like* Bill Blake, you know, though no one seems to have discovered that . . . there is more sense, beauty, mystery and charm in any ten selected Romany vocables than in the whole of the doubly damned symbolism of W.B.

He wrote again to Raleigh at Christmas the same year: 'Somehow or other the Gypsy side of my life looms big nowadays. Whenever I catch myself thinking of myself (a vile habit) it is as a Gypsy – not any other kind of Scholar.' And so the Rai kept returning to the gypsies, slipping away from university and family to their camps on the edge of Liverpool.

Their hospitality was a colourful contrast to academic formalities. In around 1900 Lawrence Townsend had entertained the Rai at Cabbage Hall when the Rai had asked him to cook some *otchi-witchies* (hedgehogs, a gypsy delicacy) for himself and a friend. Lawrence set out with some other gypsies to catch eight hedgehogs, which he and his wife then displayed on a damask cloth on the floor of the tent. The two Rais, wearing tail-coats, bow ties and coloured handkerchiefs sticking out of their breast pockets, sat down to eat, and the meal continued until the gypsies began to quarrel. At that point, Sampson recalled, the *prastemengros* (policemen) arrived, drawing their truncheons and breaking up the happy party.

The Rai relished the gypsies' vocabulary as much as their company. His friend Glyn Davies described how he came across him one day in Pwllheli, 'rolling along one of its crooked streets', on his way to an inn in the company of two gypsies shouting Romani at each other.

> Suddenly Sampson seemed to be overcome by an immense emotion: he stopped dead and bawled out, almost *'flebili sermone'*: 'Oh, Davies! did you hear him use the ablative – how perfectly beautiful!' I see Sampson now, face lit up, with his bad hat and with his shirt hanging over his trousers, like a blown-out topgallant not sheeted home. It was then I realized what a passion linguistics could arouse.

Such enthusiasm for gypsies and their language was now spreading further. The original club of the Romani Rais, the Gypsy Lore Society, had been in abeyance since its journal had ceased publication in 1892; but at the end of 1906 the Rai discussed its possible revival with his friend David MacRitchie in Edinburgh. They were fortunate in finding an ideal Honorary Secretary in the shape of a prosperous sugar refiner in Liverpool, Scott Macfie, who was to become a lifelong friend of the Rai. A tall, loose-limbed man of about forty with a gentle voice, he possessed a lively mind. That and an insatiable curiosity had led him to react against a Presbyterian background. Delighting in a Scots proverb, 'Every Macfie is a Gypsy', he had been inducted by the Rai into gypsy studies. Though he continued to run the family sugar business, his bachelor lifestyle was eccentric. In September 1899, after staying with him, the Rai had written to Raleigh:

> Mac's is a funny household. He keeps a housekeeper, her husband, and five sons and they form a sort of socialistic community. The boys have to be in by half past twelve. If they are not Mac roams about the streets until he finds them. He says he is trying to form their character or something . . . Macfie lives entirely on eggs.

But Macfie was both scholarly and businesslike: he provided funds to have the journal well printed and his house in Hope Place became the Society's headquarters. He insisted that every important article should be 'written by scholars for scholars'; but he also believed that 'a Gypsy journal should never be quite serious, and Gypsy lore ought to be a sort of scholarly playground'. Both Macfie and the Rai were well-placed to attract a keen new generation of writers and scholars; and when David MacRitchie launched the new series of journals in 1907 he emphasized that there was 'a strong and vigorous contingent ready to prosecute these studies still further'. The contributors were an odd bunch, including diplomats like Bernard Gilliat-Smith who became British Consul at Sofia; clergymen like George Hall, the 'Gypsy's Parson', and Canon Ackerley;

and academics like Donald MacAlister and George Grierson. But the standards were high.

Grierson (later Sir George Grierson, OM), who was in the midst of compiling his monumental *Linguistic Survey of India,* was the most formidable, for at the time philology commanded its greatest prestige, linked as it was to an imperial purpose and to understanding distant tribes who were important to the 'Great Game' for the control of India. He was the authority on the Dardic group of languages spoken in the remote valleys of the Upper Indus, whose archaic forms he believed were related to the Romani dialects of Europe – a link which the Rai dared to contradict.

The Rai's associations with dedicated scholars gave a misleading picture of respectability. His close friendships with the gypsies themselves were professionally acceptable, but it had also become clear that he had a roving eye for other girls. In this he was encouraged by Augustus John who openly defied conventional morality. John had an artist's licence for his promiscuous and virtually bigamous life; when his mistress Dorelia gave birth to his son Pyramus he assured her that 'I'm quite certain there is no penalty attached to having a bastard in the family.'

And Liverpool University, which was to receive its full charter in 1904, presented new temptations for a philandering professor: for more female undergraduates were coming in – eighteen of them in 1900. The girls were academically impressive, especially in English. From the 1860s onwards the best girls' schools had become strongholds of the teaching of English literature, which was thought to be too unmanly and too arty for boys (at Marlborough the English master rated below the dancing master). In time English literature became more acceptable to the academic world of the universities, but at the price of being stiffened with grammar and syntax. 'When literature *was* finally smuggled into the older universities,' wrote John Gross, 'it came heavily disguised as philology.' And philology provided a special opening for the well-educated 'new women' who were denied many formal careers. The *Oxford English Dictionary* made great use of scholarly spinsters and dutiful daughters who could only study at home: two Liverpool sisters, the Thompsons, supplied over 15,000 quotations for the dictionary and found corresponding with a strange gentleman – the editor James Murray – quite a dashing experience.

In Liverpool the philological emphasis had been strengthened after Walter Raleigh was succeeded as professor of English literature by Oliver Elton, an Icelandic scholar who became an admirer of the Rai – he later wrote his life in the *Dictionary of National Biography*. Together with Kuno Meyer they presented a formidable philological trio. And many of the 'new women' were attracted to philology.

The Rai was able to cast a powerful spell over them. He was an enthusiast for poetry; he was a learned grammarian; and he could initiate them into the magical Romani kingdom. And behind his ponderous style he would suddenly reveal an affectionate and passionate nature. His fellow academics were well aware that he had, as Charles Reilly put it, 'a small army of devoted women who loved him and slaved for him in helping to produce his great dictionary of Welsh Romany'. But no one realized quite how devoted they were, particularly his most loyal disciple, Dora Yates.

Dora came from a very respectable Jewish family from Germany, originally called Getz, who had been settled in Liverpool since at least the mid-eighteenth century: her father's sister was the mother of Herbert Samuel, the

Liberal politician who became Lord Samuel, with whom Dora shared holidays as a girl. Dora was the eighth child of very conservative and conventional parents. Her father, a friend of Lord Rosebery and the head of the Primrose League, had died when Dora was 7. Dora later complained that her mother had treated her with a severity and lack of affection which helped to make her a rebel. As a child she had been inspired by George Borrow with longings for the gypsy life, and the lectures of James Frazer, the anthropologist and author of *The Golden Bough* (who later became

Dora Yates at her graduation

a professor at Liverpool), heightened her interest in the folk-lore of the gypsies. She arrived at Liverpool University in 1896 as a precocious girl of 16, with a knee-length school dress and schoolgirl plaits which the young men laughed at and dipped in ink. But she was a hard-working scholar: she took a graduate honours course in English language and literature which included Gothic, Old and Middle

English. She was also fluent in French and German, taking a prize for a German essay, and her MA was said to be the first ever awarded to a Jewish woman in England.

Dora worshipped the librarian John Sampson from afar and it was not until she graduated that she came into close contact with him. While teaching English at a girls' school in Liverpool she joined his postgraduate course in bibliography. At the same time, under his instruction, both she and a small group of enthusiasts that included three other girls, Gladys Imlach (known as Damaris), Eileen Lyster and Agnes Marston (known as Kish), began to learn the Romani language. But not until they had thoroughly mastered it were they allowed to meet his gypsy friends. Inspired by the Rai's vision and deeply influenced by him, they all competed for his favours; they also all wrote in an elegant hand not unlike his; and they all remained unmarried.

By the end of 1903 Dora and Kish were considered sufficiently well-versed in Romani; and on Christmas Eve in a snowstorm the Rai – in a velvet jacket and 'disgracefully baggy' trousers – first took them to meet the gypsies, an experience Dora vividly described:

He had hired an old musty four-wheeled cab known as a 'growler', and the grumpy driver looked anything but pleased when he heard our destination was somewhere near the Black Bull, Aintree; his grumpiness increased when the Rai flung into the vehicle a pile of picturesque but worn-out garments of his own and an enormous unplucked turkey whose neck hung wrily and bloodily over the cushioned seats. Armed, however, with this fine bird, black twist tobacco and cigarettes for the men, silk kerchiefs for the girls, and sweets for the children, we felt confident of breaking through the reserve of any Gypsy camp in the world.

So when we alighted from the cab on a desolate piece of waste ground, and could just pick out some faint lights and a few murky figures through the snowstorm, we felt almost the thrill of a novitiate who first beholds with his own eyes the object of his worship. Dogs barked and children ran forward with echoed cries of 'The Rai! the Rai!' – and we were well and truly landed in a gypsy encampment.

They were welcomed by Mackenzie ('Kenza') Boswell, the head of the Boswell clan in Lancashire, who took them into his beehive tent made of hazel rods and pelts. There they presented their gifts while other gypsy friends crowded into the tent to greet the Rai. As the men exchanged stories of fighting and poaching, Kenza's daughter Alamina took Dora and Kish to her own barrel-topped gypsy wagon, full of immaculate ornaments and utensils, and told their fortunes, warning Dora that she had 'given all her luck away to another' (which may, as it turned out, have been true). Later they returned to Kenza's tent, sitting cross-legged in front of the wood fire to listen to more stories, and then to Kenza – dressed up comically in the Rai's baggy trousers – singing a famous gypsy song about his father Sylvester Boswell.

Dora and Kish had entered the kingdom that was to transform their lives. From then on they saw themselves as the Rai's disciples, always longing to help his Romani researches, joining him on expeditions and combining philology with new friendships and exotic encounters.

The Rai was still extending his Romani horizons. Sometimes Liverpool would suddenly be invaded by bands of foreign gypsies, at a time when immigration laws were more relaxed. The Rai would be alerted to their arrival by friends, or the police, and would then trace them to find out where they came from and to extend his vocabulary. On one such excursion to Wavertree Fields he was exploring a mysterious caravan when he stumbled on what he thought were chained-up dogs, but when he lit a match he discovered they were huge bears – fortunately engrossed in consuming bran-mash. The van-owner emerged, aroused by the noise, and turned out to be a bear-leader (one of the *Ursari*) from Slovakia, with whom the Rai could talk in regional Romani.

One day Liverpool's central railway station was suddenly filled with Hungarian gypsies who settled there with oriental calm until they were found a more appropriate camping-site at Aintree. And in 1906 the newspapers repeatedly reported a mysterious gypsy band moving through Britain. Unsurprisingly, gypsy scholars took a great interest in them, comparing them to the gypsy invasion of Western Europe five centuries earlier. The gypsy band wandered through Scotland and England until in July they were sighted in Blackpool, then a fashionable seaside resort where gypsies ran the fun-fairs and one of the few towns, said the Rai, where gypsies were regarded as an asset. Setting out immediately for Blackpool with Dora and Kish, the Rai found the newly arrived foreigners on the South Shore, near the tents of local gypsies. As he described the spectacle:

> Drawn up within were their long, low-set wagons, the gypsy women squatted on the ground surrounded by their half-naked progeny, while the men, black and bearded, strolled about smoking long, narrow-bowled pipes. The first indication of charitable intention on the part of any visitor was the signal for a general descent upon him by the *décolletée* mothers of Egypt, exhibiting their sucklings to excite compassion, and driving each

other away like wildfowl fighting for food thrown to them. Even sturdy, well-grown youths, looking like own brothers to our English Boswells, were not ashamed of pressing their stomachs and pointing to their mouths to signify they were hungry. In the centre of the ring, selling 'bost-karts,' was a Gypsy boy, with a droll, pathetic expression, like a circus clown sad at heart, an impression enhanced by his ridiculous dress, for he wore a red fez covered with gold braid, a scarlet jacket, and a brilliant sash emblazoned with the royal arms and a rubicund portrait of King Edward VII. In this garb, and skipping about with a fixed grin which only accentuated the ruefulness of his countenance, he looked so like an organ-grinder's jacko that it was difficult to resist casting a furtive glance for the tail which ought to have peeped out beneath his red jacket.

According to my custom when meeting strange gypsies, I made no immediate attempt to engage them in conversation, but walked around the little groups with the mien of a stolid Britisher, accustoming my ear to their guttural tones and strange accent, until I could follow their Romani without much difficulty.

The Rai was in a philologist's paradise. He soon deduced from their use of the oblique article *le* and from the words for 'not' and 'don't' that they were not speaking the ordinary German dialect, but a dialect with some Romanian influence which suggested they came from the Carpathians. Eventually he tried talking to the monkey-boy:

The effect was instantaneous. His jaw dropped, then followed an amazed stare and finally a grin which crept gradually across his face until it reached at last from ear to ear ... In a moment I was surrounded by a dozen

Gypsy men all firing off eager questions. Was I a Gypsy or a *gajikano rom*? (their equivalent of Romany Rye). What country did I belong to? And so forth. I had felt some doubt as to my capacity to maintain a conversation in an unfamiliar dialect, but these friendly greetings seemed to endow me with an unexpected volubility and command of language, so that I spoke almost as fluently and eagerly as the Gypsies themselves, quickly picking up new accents and intonations, until soon my Romani differed little from their own.

They told the Rai that they came from Prussia, but their vocabulary revealed them as cosmopolitan gypsies who included some Hungarians and Romanians. He asked whether they knew any stories; and one of them, called Laiji, began to recite the folk-tale 'The Count's Daughter'. The Rai sat cross-legged on the sand recording it in his notebook on his knee and surrounded by a noisy and inquisitive crowd, while Dora copied it in a second note-book and Kish noted Laiji's dress and gestures. Fifty years later, Dora wrote that the recital

> still remains an unforgettable experience for the collector of folk-lore. For this Gypsy audience seemed to know the tale quite as well as the story-teller himself, and when Laiji stopped suddenly, on purpose it would seem to give some other narrator a chance, one German Gypsy after another would take up the story . . .

The story was interrupted by the arrival of fifty consta-bles. Dismantling the tents and throwing them into the wagons, they towed them away with corporation horses, with the Rai, the two girls and the gypsies inside. They were taken all the way to Preston, where the Rai remained while Dora and Kish returned home to find that their parents had locked them out.

In 1910 a much more magnificent and exotic group of gypsies arrived at Birkenhead. They were Romanian coppersmiths, equipped with huge silver tea-urns, and with their own specially baked bread. Their women wore gold coins plaited in their long hair, and they could recite folk-tales entirely from memory. For the Rai they provided marvellous new material, as he wrote to Arthur Symons:

> There are some glorious Gypsies encamped now by the Mersey, Romanians by origin, but world travelled and speaking (most of them) Russian, Polish, French, German and a little Spanish and Italian, as well as their own tender and beautiful version of Romani – more beautiful falling as it does from the lips of proud and splendid men, and womankind who have indeed every element of strangeness added to their beauty. Their field is a blaze of colour, spread over with eiderdown quilts and strange hangings, un-English tents and huge copper vessels, where in and out flit the most beautiful Romani chais I have ever seen – gay, fearless, friendly, brilliant in every shade of red and yellow, their long black hair twisted in two plaits, into which are woven gold coins about the size of a two-guinea piece. They gleam and glitter in the sun, I have never seen anything like it. No such piece of pageantry was ever put upon the stage.

But the Rai's chief prey were the Wood family, who alone spoke the 'deep' Romani language and who were soon to uproot him still further. He enlisted Dora and Kish in two critical quests. The first was to track down the burial-place of Abram Wood, the great patriarch of the clan. Abram had been described in the parish register of Selattyn in Shropshire in 1715 as 'a reputed King of the Gypsies', and supposedly lived to be over a hundred. He was believed to have first entered Wales two centuries before: his great-granddaughter Saiforella, the witch 'Old Taw', had described him to Scott Macfie as a magnificent figure on horseback, wearing a three-cocked hat with gold lace, a silk coat with swallow-tails, a waistcoat embroidered with green leaves, white breeches tied with silk ribbons, and pumps on his feet with silver buckles and spurs. The buttons on the coat were half crowns, those on the waistcoat shillings. Abram was said to have been the first person to bring the violin into Wales: he and his children had travelled through the Principality, playing first the fiddle and then the harp. His descendants included generations of harpists who joined the retinues of landed families. But all Old Taw could say of Abram's final resting-place was that he was buried in a lone church by the sea, between Harlech and Towyn in Merionethshire.

At the Rai's behest Dora and Kish set off in 1907 along the coast of North Wales, looking at parish registers and searching for members of the Wood family who might give them clues. Eventually they found Eldorai, Old Taw's ugly daughter, who remembered her mother discussing how Abram died in a cowshed on the mountainside, and how his coffin was brought down through the village of Bryncrug to an old church, with harps and fiddles playing on the way. In Bryncrug Dora and Kish found a Welshman who knew all the Woods. He in turn directed them to a retired vicar in nearby Llwyngowril, who was certain that 'some ancient patriarch' was buried in the churchyard at Llangelynin, on the coast two miles away. They duly found an isolated little church by the sea, where a friendly sexton confirmed that the old gypsy had indeed been buried in the churchyard: he himself had seen the entry of Abram Wood in the register of burials. The girls were triumphant, and the entry was later found by Eileen Lyster under the date 12 November 1799: 'Abram Woods a traveling Egyptian'. Three decades later, in 1934, a sexton uncovered a gravestone in front of the porch engraved with the initials AW, which remains there to this day.

Their other assignment from the Rai was more difficult but also more important: to find Matthew Wood, the Romani source and storyteller who had so suddenly disappeared nine years before. The Rai had searched in vain, making three journeys to Wales and sending letters to post offices, vicars and police stations. In 1908 he asked Dora and Kish to take over. They first tracked down Ithal Lee, another friend of the Rai's, who was weaving baskets near Corwen. He assured them that his cousin Matthew Wood, 'the old hedgehog', was certainly somewhere near and he directed them to another cousin, Charlie Wood, who was living in a house near Barmouth. Charlie knew Matthew 'as well as his own boots' and promised to 'track the old grey badger to his lair before the week is out'. He then set off into the hills on his own, and returned two days later to tell them he had found Matthew Wood 'at the end of nowhere' – in a small village near Corwen called Bettws-Gwerfil-Goch.

Delighted at their discovery, the two girls telegraphed the Rai, who took the next train to Corwen and met them at the Cymru inn at Maerdy, two miles from Matthew's village. Then they walked up a winding lane into the hills, until they found 'a tiny scattered village which seemed to be hidden by trees and surrounded by hills'. Opposite The White Horse inn was a cottage, from which emerged a man in a black bowler hat, grey coat, purple stockings and high boots. The Rai immediately recognized Matthew and they greeted each other in deep Romani. The quest was over, and the stage set for a more lasting Bohemian adventure.

6

The Vagabond King

I T WAS IN this Welsh village of Bettws-Gwerfil-Goch, 'at the end of nowhere', that the Rai decided in 1909 to establish his own family base from which to pursue his gypsy studies. The local farmer, Thomas Thomas, showed him two adjoining houses called Cae Gwyn which he had just built on the hillside above the village, complete with bathrooms which were then a rare luxury in rural Wales. The two houses could be joined together and rented for £12 each a year. The Rai wired his wife to come and see them, and there they settled. All the furniture was brought from Liverpool in two pantechnicons, followed by the three children, Michael, Amyas and Honor, looked after by Kish and Dora, together with their maid Nellie and their dog Ashypelt (named after a Romani folk-tale). Some visitors were rude about the houses: 'He lived for some years, apparently unconscious of their ugliness, in a couple of the worst Welsh suburban villas set on a glorious hillside above Corwen,' recalled Charles Reilly, the professor of architecture.

But the Rai saw them as an enchanted eyrie: 'below the Bodynlliw woods the river Alwen wound its way to the Dee; beyond, to the south, shone the three peaks of Aran, while in the distance loomed Snowdon, the great Iveski Mura. This lovely spot was a favourite rendezvous of the Welsh Gypsies of every family.'

North Wales at the turn of the century provided spectacular contrasts between industrialization and rural agricultural life, between bleak quarries and factories and wild natural beauty. Already by 1862, when George Borrow had published his travel book *Wild Wales*, railways had made that corner of Britain much more accessible. Forty years later the network of railways along the valleys could carry English travellers into the remotest outposts – by 1897 there was even a rack-and-pinion railway to the top of Snowdon – while the Welsh emigration into Liverpool and the north of England had brought English-speakers into the remote villages. Small farmers and labourers had begun to lose their independence with the rapid accretions of a few big landowners: the biggest, Sir Watkin Williams-Wynn, based near Wrexham, owned 150,000 acres in North Wales. Many rural families lived in great poverty and squalor. But philologists from Borrow onwards were not much concerned with social problems and found the isolated valleys an ideal setting for linguistic studies.

The houses on the hill at Bettws soon became both the Sampson family home and the centre of gypsy studies and revelry. During the academic term the Rai lived in rooms in Liverpool with Michael who attended the local grammar school, the Liverpool Institute; while his wife Margaret stayed at Bettws with the younger children Amyas and Honor, joined by the Rai only for some weekends. But during the holidays the Rai presided at

Bettws over his family, his gypsy friends and his female assistants, extending his Romani vocabulary and grammar with the help of his rediscovered mentor Matthew Wood. A succession of scholars and old friends from Liverpool, including the Eltons, the Dowdalls, Kuno Meyer, Walter Raleigh and Charles Reilly, would come up from the station at Corwen and make their way to the remote village.

Augustus John.

The first entry in the visitors' book was that of Augustus John, accompanied by a flamboyant self-portrait. In October 1909 he had come up from Liverpool, where he had been painting the later notorious portrait of the Lord Mayor, Challoner Dowdall. The Rai had warned him that he had just endured 'a diabolical attack of lumbago, and can not move', but Augustus arrived at Bettws in high spirits after escaping from the stuffy town hall, and the Rai soon revived with the help of much whisky, while Augustus was delighted by the Romani entertainment.

Matthew Wood played his fiddle while Augustus sang till late in the night. But trouble followed. As John wrote to his American patron John Quinn:

> There were two young ladies present, secretaries of the Rai. After going to bed I became possessed of the mad idea of seeking one of them – it seemed to me only just that they should do something in the way of entertaining *me*. I sallied forth in my socks and entered several rooms before I found one containing a bed in which it seemed to me I discerned the forms of the two girls. I lay down at their sides and caressed them. It was very dark. Suddenly a voice started shrieking like a banshee – it might have been heard all over Wales. I thought then that I had stumbled upon Sampson's boys instead of them I sought.

In fact Augustus later realized that he had caressed the Rai's 5-year-old daughter Honor and the maid Nellie. Coming down to breakfast the next morning he was

> met at every turn by grim and disapproving looks: the little girl, Honor, alone greeted me with friendly merriment. Finding this atmosphere little to my taste, without word or ceremony I walked out of the building. I had the day before me.

Augustus walked as far as one of the inns at Bettws, The White Horse, and was making good progress with an attractive-looking Welsh girl called Blodwen when, to his surprise and annoyance, John Sampson strode in.

> The Rai announced rather pompously that upon reflection he was unwilling to allow my behaviour at

Cae-gwyn to interrupt our friendship and would overlook it. I answered shortly that I had no apologies to make, and thanked him for nothing. Upon this, with an inward struggle, he assumed a more playful tone and ordered drinks.

The two men then moved on to the other inn, The Hand, where they met up with some more gypsies of the Wood clan. The Rai was soon back in his element with songs, drink and talk of grammar. Augustus described what happened next:

Soon the inn resounded with the melodious accents of the Romani language, preserved by the Woods in a richly inflected form. Each Kalo vied with his neighbour in grammatical nicety, and solecisms were greeted with derision. The symposium was only marred by the truculent behaviour of one of the company, Howell by name. Roused to action by this graceless fellow, I took it upon myself to throw him out: a short struggle ensued which ended in the road, with Howell prone and myself astride him: dismounting I left him to be led away by his brothers, bleeding profusely: I seemed on the whole to have had the best of the encounter.

Dora Yates put a more heroic gloss on the affair:

Out they went from the inn into the sunlight of the square and stripped to the waist, and in two rounds John knocked the fellow out, giving him the licking he so thoroughly deserved and ridding Bettws once and for all of a braggart bully who never dared show his face again.

John's visits to the Rai in North Wales were doubly important to his development, for though he was himself a Welshman, brought up in Tenby before his departure to London and Liverpool, it was the Rai who taught him Welsh and opened up a more romantic aspect of the Principality. As Ceridwen Lloyd-Morgan has written in a recent study, 'Instead of the anglicised, respectable, pious, middle-class Wales of Tenby . . . he discovered a very different and far more enticing Wales, peopled with colourful characters speaking Welsh and Romani, a world full of singing, dancing, story-telling, swearing and fisticuffs.'

John brought with him to Bettws friends who shared his fascination with Wales and gypsies, among them the young Welsh artist James Dickson Innes, who had recently settled in a cottage near Mount Arenig where he was painting the mountain. Innes was thrilled by gypsies. According to Augustus he once bought and painted a caravan to receive a ravishing gypsy girl: when she preferred to stay in the village pub the romance faded and Innes left the caravan to rot. In March 1911 he visited Bettws with Augustus, staying at the Rai's eyrie where he left a drawing of a fantastic mountain in the visitors' book. Innes was already weakened by the tuberculosis which was to kill him three years later, but still he shared John's sexual adventures, obeying what he called 'the stern call of dissipation'. Augustus later described one such escapade:

> While staying with John Sampson at Bettws-Gwerfil-Goch, Innes and I one day set out for the neighbouring town of Corwen. In the bar of an inn we came across a family of Gypsies with whom we consorted. This family was of the rare tribe of Florence. One of the young women, Udina, was of great beauty, elegance and charm. All Gypsy girls are flirts and this one was no

exception to the rule. Uninured to their wiles, Innes no
less than I was deeply moved; we both secretly
established an understanding with Udina. The family
were to depart next day for Ruthin. At length,
reluctantly, we said good-night and returned to
Sampson's. The next morning Innes was not to be
found. I guessed his whereabouts. As it turned out,
stealing a march on me, he had risen early and gone
back to Corwen to rejoin the Florences, but finding
them gone had set out to overtake them on foot. On the
outskirts of Ruthin, overcome with fatigue, to which the
state of his health no doubt contributed, he had fallen
by the road-side, and was discovered in collapse by a
charitable passer-by who took him home, and kept him
in bed till he recovered. But Udina Florence, the girl of
both our dreams, was never seen again.

J. D. Innes' entry in the visitors' book at Cae Gwyn, 1911

The Rai clearly enjoyed the adventures of his visitors
and joined them in the local pubs, in Bettws, Maerdy or
Corwen. When his wife complained he rudely insisted
that he was only following his sense of duty:

Dear Girl,

I *did* mind going with John and Innes, but thought it better to go with them, and see no more bother arose in Corwen. If you knew much of me you would know how often I do things I mind (or don't like) doing. I had no pleasure in their company of which I was heartily tired though I liked meeting John again. The sleet cut my hands and gave me such acute pain that I woke and tossed awake from 12 to 5.

Augustus shared the Rai's passionate pursuit of the gypsy language. 'I want to know how you get on at Bettws-Gwerfil-Goch,' he wrote from Chelsea. 'I shan't be satisfied till I see old Matthew Wood and I look to you to get me that privilege. Your new scheme interests me enormously and I only wish I were *in it* to help – if I only had a *finger* (little one) in the *grammar* I'd die happy ...' He finished the letter on the next page, scrawling 'I've bungled the writing paper as usual – must fill it up somehow' and drawing an exuberant sketch of himself with a prancing horse.

Augustus returned to Bettws with two other drinking friends, Joseph Holbrooke and the fantastical painter David Sime. They had been staying with John at Chirk Castle as guests of the art patron Lord Howard de Walden who shared a studio in Chelsea – and other pleasures – with Augustus. The Rai's eyrie at Bettws was now on the itinerary of a small school of painters, among them the Australian painter Derwent Lees at Festiniog, and Innes at Nant Ddu, who were discovering in North Wales 'the reflection of some miraculous promised land' as Innes himself put it. Most of these visitors were interested in gypsies, as were serious scholars like E. O. Winstedt, Scott

Macfie, Bernard Pares and Oliver Elton. But there were also hints of amorous activity, including an anonymous reference in July 1913 to Mary Dowdall ('the Rani') and a mysterious Charles (Reilly?):

> Mary Dowdall yesterday
> Was Charles' earthly prop and stay.
> Oh how different today!
> What her name is who shall say?

Augustus John's ending to a letter to the Rai

Another visitor was the poet Arthur Symons, a friend and acolyte of Augustus John's, who had been inspired by the Rai's new edition of Blake to write a book about Blake himself. Symons had been attracted to the gypsies ever since a visit to Spain and easily identified with them, for he saw himself fated, after an unhappy wandering childhood, ever to remain a nomad: 'If I have been a vagabond and have never been able to root myself in any one place in the world, it is because I have no early memories of any one sky or soil. It has freed me from many prejudices in giving me its own unresting kind of freedom.'

Symons had recently gone mad in Italy and had been locked up. It was only with difficulty that he had been freed, and he was now firmly supervised by his wife Rhoda. In Wales he was enchanted by the landscape: 'I noticed the rich greenery, the waterfalls and streams, the luxuriantly wooded hills all around, with the background of Snowdon and the other peaks.'

The Rai was nevertheless relieved when the visit was over. 'I parted from the Symonses at Ruabon,' he wrote to his wife afterwards, 'Arthur being most affectionate and touching. Mrs S whom I think quite heartless I hope I shall never see again. Both of them had so got on my nerves that I felt I wanted to dismiss them from my mind for a bit.' As Augustus John later wrote, Symons and the Rai 'did not get on very well together I fear'.

A more welcome visitor was the Reverend George Hall, the rector of Ruckland in Lincolnshire. He had been fascinated by gypsies since the age of 10, when he became infatuated with a gypsy girl called Sibby Smith at his dame's school. 'Whimsical as the wind, and brimful of mischief as an elf of the wilds, Sibby was to me the embodiment of bewitching mystery.' He had pursued his interest in gypsies through his ordination, marriage and settled life in the rectory, writing a book called *The Gypsy's Parson* which, while it celebrated the gypsies, gave little indication of his religious role: 'If the gypsies possess any religion at all, it may be summed up in one sentence –

reverence for the dead.' And he explained how dead gypsies' possessions were burnt or buried to keep away the ghosts which would otherwise hover around them. Hall, like some other Romanophiles, saw gypsies as children who never grew up: 'Like nature herself, these wildlings of hers overflow with the play-spirit and therefore remain ever youthful.' Corresponding with the Rai about Romani words and pedigrees, he reassured him that 'my regard for them is such that I would not have them other than they are'.

The Rai invited Hall to stay in Wales, and went to meet him in Corwen, but suspected he was 'a trifle *mato*[drunk]' when they got into the trap: sure enough, disaster overtook them on the mountain road. As the Rai told Augustus:

He was sitting behind, and the driver said he thought he had heard one of the bags fall out. I went back and found him lying in a ditch . . . I had hoped that a parson might give an air of respectability to my cot, instead of which his general air, tattered clerical coat, huge bandage over one eye, and habit of smoking a short pipe and drinking beer in the village pub, produced quite the reverse effect.

The Rai forgave him: 'he is a good man,' he told Augustus, 'a fine Gypsy raconteur, an expert poacher and – so far at any rate as Gypsies are concerned – an approver of plural marriages'. Hall for his part was enchanted by Matthew and Harry Wood and by the Sampson family, particularly Honor to whom he told Romani tales as they scrambled up the hills. 'Let me again say – it was a blissful time away then far from the humdrum of ordinary duties. But – I'm growing sentimental.'

The Rai presided over Bettws as a kind of vagabond king. 'He had but to stamp his foot, or whatever is the Romany equivalent,' wrote Charles Reilly, 'for the tribes of gypsies to collect and dance before their Rai.' The gypsies' songs and folk-tales mixed naturally with the scholarly task of recording words for the dictionary. And it pleased the Rai to portray his visitors as outcasts like the gypsies: when Glyn Davies, working at the Library in Aberystwyth, came to stay he overheard the Rai describing him to Matthew Wood and using the word *stariben* (jail): he realized that he was being commended to Matthew as a seasoned poacher.

The most scholarly rival to the Rai was Bernard Gilliat-Smith, a younger man and an ambitious philologist. He had first become fascinated by Romani as a student in Germany when he had come across gypsies speaking a rare dialect in the woods at Sponheim, and he had begun to explore the complex local variations of Romani. When posted to the consular service in Sofia he had spent much time with Muslim gypsies, and in 1911 he published a learned paper in the Journal of the Gypsy Lore Society about the transformation of the consonants 'r' and 's' in Romani, which disposed of the theory that the word Rom was derived from the Greek *rumi*. Gilliat-Smith became an enthusiastic disciple of the Rai, who returned the compliment: as he wrote to him much later in 1926, 'When you first swam into our ken – witty yet learned – a new prospective better Borrow, I hailed you as one of the world's real Romany Ryes.' Gilliat-Smith came to stay with the Rai at Bettws in July and August 1912, and was convinced of the authenticity of the 'deep' Romani spoken by the Woods. Though he and the Rai were later to be alienated by mutual jealousy, in Bettws he was the Rai's acolyte. He adopted the name Petulengro and was photographed with the Rai, Dora and the two young gypsy sisters, Rosie Griffiths and Mary-Lizzie.

The philologists sometimes wrote about their gypsies as if they were really their creations, like Professor Higgins and Eliza in *Pygmalion*; but the Rai at least had some real gypsy friends and gained the trust of the Wood family of all generations. Rosie Griffiths was a girl of 13 when the Rai first met her near Bettws, where she was camping with her mother Rosaina and her father Feofilus, both descendants of Abram Wood who spoke deep Romani. Dora Yates described her as a 'slim graceful girl with a mane of black hair and deepset eyes'. Her father was too lazy to support the family, so Rosie helped to look after her mother Rosaina and her younger sister Mary-Lizzie, though still keeping her sense of fun and continuing to play the mouth-organ. She was a devout Roman Catholic and every year she and Mary-Lizzie went to a convent to work for a month at the laundry under unfamiliar discipline: 'Sir we feel it hard being in close confinement,' she once wrote to the Rai, 'as you know Sir a gibsey life is a happy one which you have said it yourself.' The Rai was enchanted by her, providing occasional gifts for which she was touchingly grateful: 'you're the only friend I have, more like a father'. Her looks contradicted suspicions that she might, in fact, be the Rai's daughter; but she remained a life-long friend, looking after him on his death-bed twenty years later.

The Rai had to keep the gypsies away from the university. 'Rosie and Mary-Lizzie are reported to have called at the Univ today,' he once wrote to his wife, 'a thing they were warned never to do on any account whatever. Dora was told by the porter, saw them and administered a weighty rebuke.' But he did arrange for some gypsies to come to a lecture he gave about them.'Alabaina and her sister Lily and one of the younger ones came over for it (fetched by Dora in a stipulated taxi) and enjoyed themselves immensely (except of course sitting on the chairs during the actual lecture). They were all in their best, and tremendous swells. Afterwards they did a little *drukeriben* [fortune-telling].'

Many visitors saw Bettws as part of a Bohemian idyll, with the Sampson family and helpers sitting round the Rai's caravan, mingling cheerfully with the gypsies in a wild and beautiful setting. Dora Yates later recalled:

Everyone will remember not only how Mrs Sampson presided over the whole household so imperturbably and welcomed her guests so heartily, but how good-tempered Maggie Jones would wait on them all – professors, artists and their wives, Gypsies and the Sampson children – with a wise, engaging grin on her face and a look of rapt adoration for the exploits and chatter of the five-year-old Honor, her special charge. Yes! those were spacious days of plenteous fare and cheerful, willing service!

The family did not see it quite like that, particularly Margaret Sampson, stuck in the cold, windy house for long winter months with very little money and only infrequent and unpredictable visits from her husband. The Rai wrote quite often to Dear Old Chap, Dear Darling, Dearest Girl, Dearest Kid. Occasionally he showed genuine concern. 'I don't want my work to turn me into an absolutely selfish and self-centred person', he wrote in 1914, 'and you must warn me if you see this coming on.' But he showed little interest in her own doings or feelings, recounting instead his university chores, his dinners with the Reillys or the Dowdalls, and news of visitors to Bettws, particularly the inevitable Dora, Kish and Eileen. Increasingly, too, he complained about his health – his colds, his gout, his teeth or just his 'melancholy' – implying that his wife didn't really understand him. In photographs she was already looking sadder, with a downturned mouth. And Dora later claimed that 'she would drink too much you know'.

The Sampson children certainly enjoyed the open-air life and their proximity to nature. In the summer they could camp out around Esmeralda, a bow-topped gypsy wagon with small windows on each side. Later, Honor would often talk to her own children about her happy times in Bettws. My father Michael, who was 13 when they moved there, relished the wildlife, particularly the birds: in later life he would always seem happiest when walking in the hills. As a child he impressed visitors to Bettws: 'I hear Michael sets people by the ears with his abnormal wits,' wrote Augustus. But he was a lonely boy who never found friendship easy, and during his adolescence he withdrew more deeply. He never felt close to the gypsies, never spoke of them to his children afterwards, and certainly never shared the romantic and erotic stimulus which the gypsies aroused in his father.

The air of romance that surrounded the gypsies was confused with fantasy. Gypsy girls were much less accessible than they looked: they could be tantalizing flirts, as Augustus discovered, but their morals were often strict. Yet the aura which surrounded them and their remoteness from normal conventions and rules acted on their admirers like an aphrodisiac, laced with the Romani language. The Rai began to write Romani poems which conveyed his own excitement. (The Oxford University Press published them twenty years later, together with his rather embarrassing translation.) 'What primitive lust and irony in them!' commented Arthur Symons, who especially enjoyed one poem entitled 'Nether Things' which began 'Beneath thy dainty black eyebrows thine eyes scan me/Like my dear God's fires which search the soul within me'. Another, 'The Five Wives', seemed to conjure up the Rai's fantasy life:

I have five wives, whom I love passing well: and so, please God, may it be to the end of my life.

One I wedded in church, another over a branch of broom, one on the river-bank, one in a woodland glade, and one in a straw-thatched hut.

And when the hour strikes, and it is time for me to go, all five will grieve for me in their five different ways.

Were the five wives pure fantasy? The Rai's friends often speculated about his female assistants or secretaries – whether at Bettws or in Liverpool. His four most recognizable 'disciples' – Dora Yates, Agnes Marston ('Kish'), Eileen Lyster and Gladys Imlach ('Damaris') – seemed equally devoted to Romani and the Rai. Dora and Kish had shared many gypsy adventures with the Rai. Kish looked very Norse, with deep grey eyes – as Dora described her, 'a graceful shy girl like a lovely, wild bird and almost as elusive and reserved as the gypsies themselves'. Dora was the more serious philologist, inducted by the Rai into the discipline of bibliography though not, as it turned out, as single-minded as she appeared.

Eileen Lyster was much more frail and neurotic, and her spelling and grammar were shaky. The Rai described her to Glyn Davies as 'the greatest possible help to me in turning out Blake – absolutely accurate, one of the sort of people who are incapable of incorrectness'. But the Rai had also been seen with Eileen outside the university precincts, and when Glyn Davies joked about it the Rai had to ask him not to mention it further, particularly to Kuno Meyer: 'he is rather a gossip and a little inclined to *elfishness* – a queer delight in being gently mischievous'.

The Rai relied heavily on the unpaid help of these eager female students for much of his research and he longed for a bigger staff. 'I sometimes dream of an "Arts Laboratory",' he told Davies, 'with about a hundred workers, under proper instruction. My God! What results one could achieve!' He looked with envy at Oliver Elton, the professor of English who had far more female students at his lectures who could have been mobilized. 'What couldn't I do with them!' But were his ambitions purely professional?

Dora, Kish and Eileen frequently came down to Cae Gwyn during vacations and at weekends. And during term-time the Rai often mentioned them in his letters to his wife, coming in and out of his rooms, helping him with his research or looking after him if he felt ill, which he frequently did.

The fourth disciple Gladys Imlach was much less in evidence. The Rai called her 'Damaris' – after the daughter of the gypsy patriarch Abram Wood – because he disliked her first name. She achieved one early distinction: in 1907 she wrote a book, *Freda's Fortune*, which was published by Jack in Edinburgh. A tale of a girl befriended by gypsies, it was accompanied by drawings of Romani families beside caravans or camp-fires, and captions such as 'Look at the darling Gypsies!' Though it was mawkish the Rai recommended it to friends, including George Hall who dutifully wrote back that '*Freda's Fortune* has been read with real delight by every member of our household . . . Miss Imlach will be pleased to hear this, and we look for new Gypsy tales from her pen.' But Miss Imlach was never mentioned in the Rai's letters and never appeared in the visitors' book at Cae Gwyn.

The Rai's close friends were well aware of his philandering tendencies, and some of them enjoyed writing him bawdy letters. Kuno Meyer once began a letter with the limerick:

> There was a young lady of Harwich
> Who immediately after her marriage
> Sewed up her chemise
> From the neck to the knees
> That she might not be —— in the carriage.

Walter Raleigh thanked the Rai for sending him a 'Sunday School Teachers' Guide to Copulation' which he found 'splendid'; and he enjoyed teasing the Rai about his past escapades, even after he was married. 'Scourge of the Uncircumscribed!' he began a letter to him in August 1901,

> I have often wondered why no-one has written a full history of thy love-affairs. They were so simple and antique. 'And Samson went down to Timnath and saw a woman . . . And he came up, and told his father and mother, and said, . . . "I have seen a woman . . . now therefore get her for me to wife." Then went Samson to Gaza, and saw there a harlot, and went in unto her. And it came to pass afterward that he loved a woman in the valley of Sorek.'

In belonging to the Gypsy Lore Society (or the Gypsy Love Society as one newspaper was later to call it) both the Rai and Augustus John displayed an ulterior motive. The Society's Journal of October 1909 included an article by William MacLeod in which he described an encounter with a passionate gypsy girl: 'She took my hand, placed it against her body and held it firmly there with both hands . . .'. The article continued in the same vein though concluding: 'it was doubtless just another case of the sensuous appeal, as with the Spanish dancers, and no indication that the Gypsy maidens are less moral than they used to be'. The Rai was fascinated: 'How did you like young MacLeod's article in [the] last number?' he asked Augustus: 'It ought to bring us in more lady members.' And in the same letter he discussed new lady members of the Society as if they were potential prey:

I saw to my astonishment that Violet Indigo Blue has joined our gang. This makes another of our old friends – though personally I have not seen her for a blue moon, and doubtless she joined to agitate either you or Macfie . . . I wonder sometimes who Miss Alice Gillington belongs to – you perhaps? – or whose Dona is Miss Torr. I think it would be more seemly if all these ladies appeared as 'Mlle X'. By the way we have a new maid.

Augustus was especially well placed to observe how the Rai, hiding behind his professorial façade, would suddenly pounce. On one visit to Liverpool with a young woman companion, he visited the gypsies at Cabbage Hall, travelling in a cab with the Rai.

A distinct but not a painful pressure applied locally to my person convinced me that someone had blundered.

Addressing myself to the corner opposite our companion, where I judged the Librarian to be sitting, I remarked conversationally, 'By-the-by, Raia, that's my leg you know.' This information was received in silence, but the pressure was instantly relaxed ...

John relished his amorous rivalries with the Rai. Years later he recalled one such incident:

When we went up to Cabbage Hall to visit the tents I was accompanied by a young lady and he too had his partner, a charming girl. We got to the tents and had some pleasing conversation with the Gypsies. I was interested in Sampson's friend who was rather beautiful. I wanted to study her and therefore persuaded her to come along somewhere where we could sit down and have a little conversation which we did. In fact we found a jolly little pub. We had a glass and some nice conversation while I had a good look at her nose and other features. Upon arriving back, I found Sampson in a bit of a state, you know. He said, 'Augustus, don't you know that I am responsible for this young lady?' However, I didn't like his attitude at all. I didn't approve of this way of speaking to one. I said, 'I don't know what your responsibilities are, but if you want to have a fight, here I am.' I said, 'Square it up, then. Ready?' He regarded me thoughtfully with a cold eye for a moment and said, 'Well, old chap, I think on the whole we'd better go and have a drink,' and I was all for it. I said, 'After all, old chap, it's all very well for you to talk about my interviewing your girlfriend but what about mine? I have had the faith in you so far to leave her in your company meanwhile so we are pretty well quits.'

Augustus also enjoyed relating stories about his philandering friend. He told W. B. Yeats – who had already
met the Rai – about the 'old reprobate professor' who was
an 'authority on gipsy lore', and Yeats passed the story on
to his American patron John Quinn in 1907:

> The old professor had a series of flirtations unknown to
> his wife, but one day when he was in a half-intoxicated
> state in a Welsh tavern where he had been studying
> gipsies he was plunged into a deep depression because
> a gipsy told him he was getting bald at the top of his
> head. 'What shall I do?' he said to John. John replied
> sternly, 'Return to your innocence', by which he meant
> sin openly and scandalise the world . . .

It was all very well for Augustus to advise the Rai to sin
openly. In the code of the time an artist might be granted
a licence for adultery – a licence which John exploited to
its limits – but academia had much stricter standards
governing the morality of dons. (Even twenty years later a
brilliant young lecturer at Cambridge, William Empson,
would be sacked because a college servant had found
some condoms in his pocket.) In straitlaced Liverpool any
evidence of adultery – particularly with gossips like Kuno
Meyer to spread it – would have meant certain dismissal
from the university. The Rai dared not tell his most
dangerous secrets to his intimate friends – even, it turned
out, to his closest hunting partner, Augustus. And for
almost a century his tracks remained covered.

Of the four disciples Dora, his trusted assistant, always
in and out of his office on business, was most obviously
the closest. The relationship appeared strictly professional
– a colleague would recollect the Rai saying at the
beginning of an important interview, 'Please leave us,

Miss Yates.' Dora was to remain discreet and loyal to the Rai who came to depend on her to the point of borrowing money: in 1919 he wrote her an IOU for £500, 'to be paid out of his estate', which she duly filed away with no record of the sum being paid back. She eventually became the Rai's literary executrix, devoting much of her life to collecting and guarding his copious papers. When my mother called her the 'wretched Dora' she implied a dragoness rather than an enchantress.

But when Dora established the Sampson Archive in the university after my grandfather's death she also included secret papers which she knew would give a very different picture to posterity. In a file labelled 'miscellaneous verse', she kept three poems in the Rai's very legible handwriting which must have been written in about 1906 – twelve years after he had married. The first was a mock dedication to the Romani dictionary on which all his disciples were working. It could have been written to any of them, but Dora did not have curls.

DEDICATION

To her who since this work began
Has fanned it with each curl,
To her who is my right-hand man
And eke my left leg girl.

The other two were clearly written to Dora. One was a more conventional love-poem, in seventeenth-century style, making play with Dora's Jewish ancestry and beginning:

Fair flower of Palestine, to thee
My thoughts tonight turn wistfully,
My heart holds thine eternally . . .

The other was a much more explicit and bawdy doggerel beginning 'Come let us write some lines on Dora'. By the third stanza it comes down to basics, Romani words providing a coded language:

> O dear, O sweet, O lovely Dora
> As all these memories I renew,
> My – call it 'presser', dear, or 'borer'
> Stands as a monument to you.
> I think of you with your dear feet up
> And minjie an inviting feast
> But now alas! you've got your street up
> And kar must wait three days at least!
>
> So now I'll end this doggerel, Dora,
> With love to you as I began,
> Love which is ever more and more a
> Reality, as I'm a man –
> As I'm a man and wear a Kari,
> As you're a girl and sport a Minj
> May I be damned or dead or hoary
> Ere I forget sweet Fanny's fringe.

Alongside the last four bawdy lines the official stamp of the University Library ensured its preservation. The Rai must have had some doubts as to how Dora would receive it:

> I wonder if you'll like this, Dora,
> Kish says you won't but then who knows ...

He need not have worried. For Dora not only kept it, but replied in kind with bawdy verses which she preserved in her notebooks in her own archive in the University Library:

Always merry is the kari
Always doing funny things
Mutering, karying, cumering minjes
Always doing funny things

Always cheerful is the minjie
Always doing funny things
Mutering, gaping, biting, coming
Always doing funny things.

There were also four stanzas about the absurdity of respectability, each one ending with the cry 'Yah!', and concluding:

Is it respectable to lie
With legs extended to the sky,
And semaphore the powers on high?
Yah!

All this was a long way from the formalities of 'Please leave us, Miss Yates'. The verses suggested a passion which put the Rai's earlier love-letters to Margaret, his 'kiddums' or 'chylde', in the shade. Both partners conveyed a heady blend of sex and scholarship, with Romani as the code and catalyst. As the Rai described his own rapture:

O blest Prof Kar to have as scholar
Miss Minj who passes double first.

7

The World Falls Apart

THE FIRST WORLD WAR shattered many of the assumptions of the gypsy dream. The philologists and eccentric amateurs were co-opted into the war effort, the travellers were conscripted and regimented in barracks which prevented their wanderings and undermined their language, and the internationalism of both gypsies and scholars was torn apart by the rival patriotisms which divided Europe and which cast suspicion on all unconventional activities or groups.

However wayward the Rai's private life, the outbreak of war in August 1914 filled him with patriotic fervour. The cosmopolitan tolerance of Liverpool and its university was soon threatened by xenophobia. In May 1915 there was an outbreak of raiding and looting of German shops in the town. 'I went to my usual place to be shaved this morning', the Rai told his wife on 14 May, 'and found it smashed and boarded up; though I hadn't known it was German . . . One can't blame the people very much. One place in Mill Street where sailors' wives denuded a pork-butcheress was due to an unfortunate jest of hers. Someone asked for black puddings and she said with a grin that they hadn't enough English blood yet to make them.'

Even before the war the growing tensions between Britain and Germany had begun to threaten the international camaraderie of the philologists. The most tragic victim was Kuno Meyer, the German professor in Liverpool who had been the Rai's loyal patron and friend, who became torn between his cosmopolitan scholarship and his surge of German patriotism. In 1910 he had accepted the chair of Celtic philology in Berlin and his Liverpool colleagues had said goodbye to him with genuine sadness. He had been at Liverpool for twenty-seven years. They commissioned Augustus John to paint his portrait, though Kuno complained that it was 'a strange production, frightfully unconventional. Open shirt, one button of the trousers open (this I must really get him to change), a red tie which I never wear, no waistcoat &c.' For all that it was one of John's finest portraits, conveying all Kuno's forceful enthusiasm. At a farewell supper, the Rai read out a mock-heroic elegy:

> Kuno is going – hence these strains of woe!
> These sad secretions of ophthalmic brine!
> Kuno is going – all our great men go . . .

The two friends missed each other. A few days before the Rai's fiftieth birthday in March 1912 he wrote Kuno a long letter: 'I wake up in the morning and murmur "Dear K.M, I will write to him to-day." I repeat this at lunch, and after dinner draw out your letter, re-read it, fall a-musing on old times, call for pen and paper, light my pipe and think affectionately of you instead of writing.' The Rai went on to reflect self-indulgently on his own fifty years: his lack of bitterness, his indifference to money, his handful of close friends. He had even enjoyed his younger days of hardship when he worked for 120 hours a week. But he often longed to escape to the gypsies and recalled one moment of total despair:

> On three several occasions at different periods of my life I have seriously thought of cutting adrift from civilisation altogether, and either adopting the life of the Gypsy, or betaking myself to some earthly paradise like Samoa; and even now this idea sometimes tugs at my heartstrings, though I have now perhaps passed the age to do it with much success. Once in my life, for reasons which I will not enter upon, I contemplated, fairly and squarely, a still more absolute removal from this scene of activities, though fortunately the occasion for this step did not arise.

Kuno replied with equal intimacy, lamenting his absence from Liverpool. 'I am not very happy here, almost the first time in my life that I feel so. I have left too many good old friends behind and I can take no interest in the affairs of institutions and people here.' But he was already fully committed to the German cause. 'It was in the summer of 1911 that I lost all hope of peace between England and Germany,' he explained three years later. And in October 1911 he had written from Leipzig to his friend Richard Best in Ireland: 'There is an extraordinary bitterness in Germany against England, which may well lead to war if it gets further nourishment.'

When war broke out Kuno wrote to the Rai from Rotterdam with the boyish excitement that at first overwhelmed both sides. 'Don't you feel you are having the time of your life, or rather that the whole world from creation onwards was not in it? Every day some new surprise, pleasant or unpleasant, but always exciting . . . Romanes must appear played out to you now as Celtic does to me.' He had come to Rotterdam, he explained callously, to record folk-tales from Belgian refugees – 'a fine study for a folklorist . . . While professors of international law have shut up their books, psychologists and folklorists have a high time of it.'

But the philologists themselves were soon at war. In November 1914 Kuno set sail for New York, ostensibly to lecture on Irish literature, but also to appeal to German and Irish Americans to support the German war effort. In New York he gave a speech to the Irish nationalist group Clan na Gael, in which he foresaw Germany invading England, winning the war and giving Ireland her independence. The London *Times* was outraged that he was using his reputation as a Celtic scholar to stir up sedition in Ireland, at the same time betraying a country to which he owed so much. Kuno replied: 'You talk cheap sentiment and false morality while two mighty Empires are engaged in a life and death struggle.' And in a letter to the Rai he warned that 'England does not realise even yet what is at stake.'

Kuno's old colleagues at Liverpool were as outraged as *The Times*. The Rai wrote to Kuno, making the break:

And so goodbye. If I hated this war for no other reason, I should hate it because it has been the means of uprooting such an old, deep and strong feeling as my friendship with you.

He went on to pillory Kuno publicly in a letter to *The*

Times, explaining that Kuno, for all his devotion to Celtic studies, regarded the Irish themselves as 'an ill-balanced, emotional race, unfitted for any form of self-government'. Deeply hurt Kuno replied, refusing to break off the friendship and calling to his aid the gypsies:

> Suppose England were at war, and at a war for life and death, with your friends the Gypsies, and called on you as a loyal subject to place your unique knowledge of the enemy at the disposal of the government, what would you do? Decline? retire? skulk? Puzzle out this conundrum for yourself, but don't tell me that if you did as I have done, you would feel less friendly to your old pals, or sever formally, as you have now done to me, and as Elton has done, so many ties of friendship, which should have stood a much severer strain.

The Senate of the University of Liverpool condemned Kuno as an agent of sedition who was 'indebted to our country for hospitality and honour'. 'I hope you are not one of those who voted for my condemnation,' Kuno wrote to the Rai. 'It is a ridiculous document which I shall take care to make widely known as a good example of the state of feeling and opinion in England ... Hospitality made me laugh. Think of Alsop's, Dale's, Rendall's hospitality!'

Liverpool professors joined in the denunciation. 'Strong's letter is the most abject, Legge's the silliest, yours the wickedest,' Kuno wrote to the Rai from Milwaukee on 7 April. 'The fatuousness of some of the others is almost grotesque. From almost all that reaches me from England I see that the sickening pharisaism and hypocrisy which we have so often studied together are now rampant throughout.' Even Augustus John was convinced, as he

117

told his American patron John Quinn, that Meyer had been spying for Germany in Liverpool; and he cabled Kuno asking for the loan of his portrait. 'I hope they won't cut it to pieces,' Kuno wrote to the Rai. In fact it was taken down from the walls of the University Club and later seized as alien property (it now resides in the National Gallery of Ireland in Dublin, regrettably in the cellar). 'It is well to remember how disgracefully even a university can behave in such circumstances,' wrote Charles Reilly, looking back on the episode in 1938 in the shadow of another impending war.

Even Kuno's Irish friends were turning against him. He wrote cordially to his old friend George Moore, describing his Irish encounters in America; but Moore sent a venomous reply concluding: 'It is hardly necessary for me to add that I am taking leave of you for ever, but not because of the German that is in you, but because of the man that is in you' – a reply which he then sent to the press. 'A fine artistic exhibition of horse-whipping', the Rai noted with pleasure.

Kuno went on writing to the Rai, and sending cuttings in German, but received no reply. The Rai told his wife in March 1915 that Kuno was 'talking still about the invasion. It is difficult to believe that he himself can believe it.' In America Kuno was having his own dramas: he was seriously injured in a rail crash in California, fell in love with a nurse of 27 and subsequently married her. 'My life is full of interest and adventure,' he wrote in December 1916, 'I hope you and yours are all well and not taking things too seriously.' Four months later he suggested that the Rai might systematically investigate gypsy settlements in Chicago and San Francisco.

After America joined the war against Germany, in April 1917, Kuno was granted a safe-conduct to return to

1. John Sampson with some disciples, *circa* 1912: Dora Yates
and Bernard Gilliat-Smith sit on the bench with John Sampson
behind them and Mary-Lizzie (*right*) and her sister
Rosie Griffiths beside him

2. The scholar as Bohemian: Kuno Meyer, the great German philologist, by Augustus John

3. The poet 'ravaged like a battlefield': Arthur Symons, by Augustus John

4. Esmeralda Lock, the gypsy singer and dancer, in Prestatyn in 1920

5. The timeless face of the old gypsy, fixed 'against the wind and open sky'

6. Matthew Wood, who taught the Rai the deep Romani language

7. Matthew's son Harry 'Turpin' Wood, who played 'the devil's tune'

8. John Sampson, near retirement

9. Dora Yates, the Rai's chief disciple, in later age, about 1937

10. Harry Wood and Rosie Griffiths with violins at the Rai's funeral

Berlin – with the help, he claimed, of a letter from his friend Lloyd George. When the war ended in November 1918 he faced the full misery of defeat, in poor health after a diet of turnips and bad bread. He tried to pick up his international interests and old friends, including the Rai:

> No amount of boiling blood, impotent rage, horror, despair during days of misery and sleepless nights has ever made me think unkindly or indifferently of old friends, who have the misfortune to belong to those nations which have brought all this on us.

The Rai evidently did not reply. Walter Raleigh, Kuno's one remaining friend in Liverpool, warned him that 'facts and events are too strong to allow an immediate and sincere resumption of former friendly relations'. Kuno replied: 'You know I am not a pessimist . . . but the future to me is pitch-dark.' He realized he would probably never return to his beloved England again. A month after that letter was written he died following an operation in Leipzig. He was 61.

'Poor old Kuno!' the Rai wrote to his son Michael with belated sympathy: 'These times since the war broke out must have been a terrible wrench to all his old feelings of friendship, and devotion to scholarship.' And he told his wife how Kuno 'was thrust into a false position, and must have known he was playing a game he knew nothing of, and have suffered constantly in heart and health and all finer feelings, and yet kept up a brave show to the last'.

While Kuno Meyer's tragic end epitomized the crumbling of international links among the Romani scholars, the war hemmed in the free movement of the gypsies themselves across Europe, as they faced military service. In North Wales the Wood family reacted to the new restrictions in different ways. Some avoided conscription through their involvement in agriculture. Others already possessed a military tradition. Ernest France Roberts, a cousin of the Wood family, had been a regimental harpist in the Boer War, and in the band of the South Wales Borderers. In the First World War many of the Woods saw in the army a unique opportunity to travel abroad: the Rai's disciple Eileen Lyster was even able to correspond with her friend Jim Wood who was serving as a soldier in Macedonia. But they were inclined to resent the restrictions of military life, and some were regularly confined to barracks. One of the Woods shot off a finger to ensure he could not fire a rifle, but at least two of the family were killed in action and another, Adolphus Wood, was found frozen to death in a trench in Belgium, still holding his rifle.

In wartime the Rai kept up his interest in gypsies. At Christmas in 1914 he collected together thirty of his Romani poems including 'Five Wives' for possible publication: they were 'the best things I have ever written in this dear language of ours,' he told Augustus John, who then agreed to contribute 'an appropriate *Walpurgisnachtstraum* illustration'. Matthew Wood still moved in and out of Bettws. 'Old Mat is back and we all work at Romani,' the Rai wrote from Cae Gwyn to his son Michael, 'getting, every now and then, a new word or form.' But the gypsy's movements were unpredictable. 'No word from Mat. I wish he had called round,' Augustus complained to Margaret Sampson from Chelsea.

The university was reduced to its bare essentials by the war. 'I'm sorry that Liverpool is busting up,' wrote Walter Raleigh to the Rai in June 1918, 'I thought it a bit shaky when I was last there. God knows how it survived its Principals.' In the library the Rai had to make do with incompetent assistants, culminating in a young man called Grimsditch – 'my last ditch' – 'a spoiled and not very attractive youth, pampered by an equally unattractive parent'.

The Rai soldiered on with his giant dictionary. 'Last Monday I finally completed the Romani vocabulary,' he wrote to Michael in the autumn of 1914, 'the work of more years than I care to contemplate, and began at once on the phonology – a stonier and more arid field.' He liked to describe his progress on the dictionary in military terms. 'My last "push" began in September,' he told his wife as he began his assault on reflexive verbs, 'and since then has resembled rather closely the progress of a campaign and taking with great efforts village after village.' By March 1916 he had overcome word-formation and was attacking inflection. By September of that year he had conquered the imperative and was advancing on the present tense. By January 1917 he had surmounted the evolution of Romani from Sanskrit and in July he at last sent 'half a hundred-weight of solid philology' to the Oxford University Press who had long before agreed to publish it, only to hear that they would postpone publication until after the war.

The Gypsy Lore Society was crippled when its chief organizer and backer Scott Macfie went off to France to become a colour sergeant in the trenches at the age of 46. In spite of his altered circumstances he retained his zest and philologist's ear. As he wrote to the Rai in November 1914:

It has been, and is, a struggle to escape being pipped for my age and other infirmities (I'm above any legitimately acceptable age and suffer in a beastly way from the cold) but I wouldn't miss it for anything . . . Couldn't you write a decent (or indecent) song for us? The men sing mostly 'It's a long way to Tipperary', but even they recognise the inanity of the words and change them to 'It's the wrong way to tickle Mary'. This might be supposed to indicate taste, but it doesn't. The verses they invent themselves are as silly as any popular ditty:

> When the English and the French
> Meet together in a trench
> It's hell for Emp'ror William.

In August 1915 the Rai reluctantly agreed to become the Society's President but he was not impressed by the new secretary, the Reverend Frederick Ackerley – 'a rather dull clergyman, about my own age perhaps, grave and careful, and not very lively', he told his wife. 'Didn't know Romani when he heard it, like most of our members.' Ackerley resigned four years later, having, as the Rai complained, 'done exactly nothing'. After Macfie returned from France in poor health he met with the Rai and others to 'consider how the poor Humpty Dumpty of the Gypsy Lore Society may be put together again'. But eventually they decided to wind it up.

The Rai's wartime patriotism was fortified by his pride in his two sons. He had always been intensely ambitious for Michael, who showed great promise as a schoolboy at the Liverpool Institute. He shared lodgings with him – a difficult constraint for a shy boy – and was concerned for his manliness, particularly when a Mr Hall suggested that Michael should join a party of boys who went to his bungalow during the holidays. When Hall called at the lodgings one evening, expecting to find Michael, he got short shrift from the Rai, who related the encounter to his wife:

> I thought it all – his look, his manner, everything rather unpleasant – most of all perhaps his want of any decent manly feeling or indignation at being so received (*which was due to his looks*) and his trying to insist on shaking hands with me on leaving. The man had a very low type of face, small head, shifty eyes and not a single scrap of the fine look of an athlete, however un-intellectual. I am deeply thankful that I chanced to see him and stop the acquaintance.

Soon afterwards the Rai was relieved by news of athletic activity: 'Glad Michael has taken to manly sports. I have always tried to encourage him to.'

As soon as the war broke out the Rai's first concern was that Michael, who was 18, should join up as quickly as possible. He was about to go up to St John's College, Cambridge, to read science, and had been awarded a scholarship. But the Rai was impatient: 'It is difficult to think or write of anything except the war.'

Michael lost no time in enlisting. By December he had a commission in the King's Royal Rifles and was beginning four months' training in Kent. There he came across a family of gypsies, the Drapers, whom he surprised by talking some Romani, but he was struck by their lack of patriotism. Mrs Draper, looking at his army uniform, said, 'I lay you wish you were out of it, young man', and she told him how her apparently healthy son was 'unfit to serve on account of consumption'.

When Michael arrived in the trenches in June 1915 his father claimed to envy him, showing the same kind of boyish enthusiasm as had Kuno: 'I wish I could have been with you,' he wrote, 'it seems strange to me that I should be here now as usual, correcting proofs and working at phonetics while you are in the thick of it. I find myself wishing that I could cross the water, and get, at any rate, near enough to the war zone to have a sniff of the war at first hand.' Ten weeks later Michael was slightly wounded and returned to recuperate – first to Bettws, then to a hospital in Dublin. He was soon back at the front, in time for the autumn offensive at Loos – the 'futile carnage' as Lloyd George later described it. 'This is glorious news for England,' the Rai wrote to his wife on 25 September: 'I hope Mickie may have come through unscathed; but however that may be it is a great thing to have played a part in this victorious attack.' Soon afterwards at Loos Michael got a bullet through his left arm and was back in hospital in Dublin. The Rai was publicly brave and proud: 'I shall always be glad,' he wrote to Michael on 12 October, 'as I feel sure you must be, to think that you played a part in making this the splendid success it seems to be.' But privately he was worried. 'You looked very much upset,' his gypsy friend Rosie Griffiths wrote from Birkenhead, 'I hope there was nothing wrong. It made me proper miserable after you left. I hope you have heard from your son Michael Sampson.'

By July 1916 the Rai's mood was more sober still, when a telegram reported that Michael had been wounded again at Rochincourt. 'I have been in dread every moment of this new push,' he wrote to his wife on 5 July, 'convinced that it would be desperate and murderous for our young men, whatever the ultimate result . . . It has been torture to me to feel that any hopes of what the English may achieve is mixed up with such fears that make me wish it had never been possible. Oh I wish I knew.' But writing to Michael he suppressed any such emotion. 'Pleased to hear you got off so lightly ... a little sorry you hadn't a longer run for your money.' By December Michael was back in the trenches.

In the last year of the war Michael was covered in glory. In January he won the Military Cross; in the spring he was wounded again in the Second Battle of the Somme, earned a bar to his MC, and was promoted to Major. In October he was wounded yet again, and was gassed for the first time. His lungs were never to recover completely. When he came home to Liverpool on leave the Rai was bursting with pride, though surprised that he had not been promoted further.

Father and son corresponded regularly in equally neat handwriting. The Rai provided news about his Romani researches, but nothing about his personal relationships. Michael wrote manly letters which his father treasured, but displayed no emotion; his accounts of his harrowing war experiences were always understated and he played down his gallantry as described in the official citation of his MC. Though his father later proudly sent to the publishers Constable an account by Michael of the fighting on the Somme, their editor tactfully pointed out that 'his description seems to me very typical of the English officer at his best: i.e. that he always appears to have few personal adventures and to be hardly moved by what is going on round him. This is his great virtue, but it is not a help to the publication of his record thereafter.'

My father, like so many men of his generation, clammed up about his experiences during the war for the rest of his life. But his general reticence and isolation were, I think, the result of the traumas of the family more than those of the trenches.

Michael's younger brother Amyas seemed destined for equal glory. In June 1915, when he was still only 15 and therefore under age for military service, the Rai was trying to arrange for him to join up: 'it hardly seems fair to him to prevent his joining on a technical ground,' he wrote to Michael. Instead Amyas was sent for two years to Canada, where he worked in a bank in Gananoque, the small town on the St Lawrence River where the Rai's brothers Walter and Jim both lived. He was less academic than Michael but had a greater sense of fun, and his letters were more vivid. In Canada Amyas enlisted in the Royal Flying Corps – then in its infancy – and trained first in Toronto and then in Texas. In 1918 he was sent over to France, flying near the front: 'One night I went over in formation with some other chaps to the front line,' he wrote home on 11 June. 'I could see all the trenches zigzagging all over the place, line after line of them, and the flashes of the guns.' On 8 August he wrote exuberantly to his mother describing 'a wonderful push this morning. It will be in tomorrow's papers I expect. I don't think it will affect us very much, but I shall send you a postcard every other day for a while so that you needn't worry.'

There were no postcards: on the same day Amyas was reported missing. Like other parents during the war, the Rai took a long time to face up to his likely death. 'Am. must have pursued the retreating Germans, don't you think?' he wrote to his wife. The next month he was still trying to reassure himself. 'Somehow I feel sure that Am. is safe.' On 13 November, two days after the Armistice, he wrote to Margaret, 'I suppose we may soon hope to hear now.' Three weeks later he asked for Michael's honest view. His son could offer little hope. 'It will be about as sad an Xmas as I have experienced,' the Rai wrote to Margaret. But inexplicably he did not spend

Christmas at Bettws, where Honor – now 13 – was ill. 'Obviously it would be very unfair to suggest that Kish and Dora should come down,' he wrote on 16 December, 'and I can't help seeing that I should be in the way.' Instead he spent Christmas with the gypsies, at Earlstown and at Newton-le-Willows, and with the Wood family.

The memory of his son haunted him and he continued to hope against hope that his body or his grave might be found. When the first anniversary of the Armistice was commemorated in Liverpool by two minutes' silence the Rai wrote to Margaret: 'On Tuesday the 11th, 11th, 11th I went and stood out in the Library, but habit and incapacity to think at the King's request prevented my doing more than repeating such names of the fallen as came into my head.' He was shocked by the irreverent students in the library: 'One sandy haired girl, as if doing it deliberately, at the half-stroke of 11 began writing violently with a scratchy pen.'

With Amyas gone, Michael was all the more important to the Rai, but he had become more distant. 'Why doesn't he write to me,' the Rai asked Margaret anxiously, 'no reason is there, that you know of?' But Michael must by now have realized that the Rai was not the moral father figure that he had seemed to be. The son withdrew into his scientific studies at St John's, Cambridge. At the end of his first year he nearly accepted a research post in industry: the Rai urged him to stay on but when he did so he only got a Second, which seriously disappointed his father. Having never been an undergraduate himself, the Rai was critical of anyone who did not make the most of university. He urged Michael not to take this verdict too seriously, but added discouragingly, 'I suppose you will try to find out how and in what you failed.' Perhaps father and son had lost confidence in each other.

A year after taking his degree Michael wrote to say he was engaged – to Phyllis Seward, daughter of the professor of botany at Cambridge, who was also Master of Downing College. For all his Bohemian instincts, the Rai was relieved that his son was to marry into a respectable academic family. He felt confident that at least 'it is *not* a *mésalliance*, that she must be by upbringing and education a lady, that the Sewards must think highly of M and his prospects'. He hoped marriage would encourage Michael to settle in Cambridge with a fellowship: 'If he got it I should be proud and look forward to an FRS as the next step heavenward.' And then he asked his wife, 'Is he in love with her, or she with him?' Reading their shy letters seventy years later it is hard to be sure. Certainly their correspondence was in marked contrast to the Rai's passionate baby-talk when he was wooing Margaret, not to mention his bawdy doggerel to Dora. Michael took solace in material facts, details and plans, and only talked about his feelings awkwardly, while my mother was distressed by his withdrawal from emotion. 'I think you are curing me of rolling up in a ball like a hedgehog,' he wrote in November 1922, 'it is sheer moral cowardice really.' But in his letters he was very rolled up.

There was little of the gypsy in the Rai's attitude to Michael's wedding in Cambridge. He worried that sending out too many invitations might 'just look like asking for presents' but reflected that some of the names 'might look respectable on the affixed labels'. He wanted to invite Dora and Kish though he wasn't sure about Augustus John. But he did not try to interfere with Michael's domestic plans.

With some apprehension, the Rai accepted the Sewards' invitation to stay in the Master's Lodge before the wedding; and Michael and Phyllis were themselves apprehensive about the arrival of this rugged provincial scholar in the midst of Cambridge society. In the wedding photographs he appears in the back row, detached and quizzical in his monocle, while his wife is overshadowed by a huge hat. The mutual apprehension proved groundless: as my mother recalled, the Rai was at his most charming and friendly.

Michael had taken a job as research chemist with the newly merged chemical company ICI, which he would serve for the rest of his life. He was sent to the new nitrogen works at Billingham-on-Tees, a desolate little company town pervaded by the stench of ammonia. Michael was concerned about bringing his bride there, with good reason: moving into the small company house, 17 Mill Lane, she was lonely among the corporate wives and longed for Cambridge. Michael himself remained undemonstrative and withdrawn. To his three children, most of all to my elder sister, he appeared alarmingly distant. And he never talked about his father. The Rai was soon reconciled to his industrial son and proud of each stage in his progress. But they now met very rarely and corresponded only formally. Michael had reacted against Bohemia to construct an almost opposite life, fortified by the certainties of science and a big company and dreading family emotion. It was my mother who had to take the strain as she learnt more about the strange family into which she had married, and as the Rai's secret life began to unravel.

8

The Missing Lover

T HE CONFIDENCE OF Liverpool would never fully recover from the devastation of the First World War. The depletion of the British merchant fleet – U-boats had destroyed 3 million tons of British shipping – and increasing competition from foreign fleets spelled the end of the Mersey's supremacy. After a brief boom Liverpool faced stagnation in trade. In a city which was heavily dependent on the docks, the spectre of unemployment loomed. The great passenger shipping companies, too, were in difficulties, compounded by the crash of the Royal Mail line. And soon the Cunard liners were sailing from Southampton rather than Liverpool. The city was losing its crucial passenger link with America.

In the first year of peace Liverpool was in turmoil, disrupted by discontented ex-soldiers who had returned to find their jobs gone, by the backlash from the Irish troubles, and by a group of militant Communists inspired by the Russian Revolution. Riots and looting threatened the city with anarchy. 'We live in stirring times,' the Rai told his wife in August 1919:

> Tanks and tommies and machine guns in evidence, battleships in the river, everything except the policeman. I went last Sunday to see London Road where about half the shops have been broken into and looted, Owen Owens among them. Next night (Sunday) they returned to finish the rest off, so that now it must look ever more like a photograph of Ypres than it did when I saw it ... The soldiers take a lenient view of the looting. One man heard a tommy say to a woman staggering off with a pile of loot 'That's right, ma, get home with it.'

Nor was he reassured by signs of material progress, as motor cars and lorries roared on to the open road beloved of the gypsies and horse-drawn caravans. 'The streets are intolerable now,' he wrote the next month, 'with all sorts of motor traffic rushing about in every direction. One hears of heaps of accidents. You would hate it.'

Liverpool University was flooded by demobilized students and new academics who lacked the pioneering spirit of the pre-war years, and the Rai felt less involved. There was a brief flurry of excitement over the election of a new vice-chancellor to succeed the previous incumbent, Arthur Dale. The Rai thought the university had been on an up-swing: 'Dale was better than Glazebrook, Glazebrook than Rendall, Rendall than nothing!' Walter Raleigh put it more rudely in the style of Blake:

> Rendall, Glazebrook, and Father Dale
> Each held on to the other's tail;
> Rendall lived on chickweed and groundsel,

Glazebrook danced to please the Council,
Father Dale in an old plug hat
Played the bones on the front-door mat,
And then crept round to the back garden
To get his money and ask for pardon.

The Rai appreciated the drama of the academic election: 'Elton walks about looking mysterious and important, and as though he feared his pocket would be picked of some important secret,' he wrote to Margaret: 'He is not human enough to be a good judge of men, and the other members are not particularly good, so that I am looking forward to the worst, perhaps Ramsay Muir who has been seen in the corridors.' Eventually they chose John Adami, a physician who was rumoured to be 'an American hustler' which alarmed the Rai: 'I hope he won't have too many new and bright ideas about the Library.' But he was reassured after seeing Adami at work: 'He conveys the impression of being a man who knows precisely what he means to do, and how it should be done. I think he will take the place a long way.'

Most provincial academics in the 1920s led austere lives, necessarily dedicated to Wordsworth's principle of 'plain living and high thinking'. But the Rai's conditions seemed more spartan than most, and he constantly complained of ill-health and hardship. He lived in simple gloomy lodgings, moving from one difficult landlady to another. 'I will not say it is out of the frying-pan etc,' he wrote to Margaret after one move, 'but except for Mrs Costie's attacks of insanity I would gladly change back.' He was soon in another lodging:

A smallish sitting room, with absurdly large furniture, and chairs enough for a Committee room – most of which I have induced [the landlady] to clear out.

A. John

a caricature of
John Sampson,
The Gypsy Scholar.

Augustus John's caricature of John Sampson, the Gypsy Scholar

Colossal bronze figures on huge side board, almost reaching to the ceiling. Bed which hardly lets you have room to walk round it, and above my head 'The Lord bless thee, and keep thee'. Food in a crude state. At lunch 2d of ham evidently just bought from some shop round the corner . . . But really it is all right, though I think I must move again.

Sometimes he found some compensation in philological research:

This morning little Mr Dadley came in at 7 as usual, with hot water for the Kutnow, and a cup of tea, and began (as usual) to describe the weather in his fine Oxfordshire – not Oxford! – accent.

'A naice faiine braiight day today, sir. You'll enjoy it. And taiime we had some good weather at last.' (deposits tray. Then going to the window and pulling up the blinds): 'OOO Laard! Raiining again worse than ever! Pelting cats and dogs!' And so it was.

He spent hardly anything on clothes: 'I am wearing an old dark grey suit, which emerged from a trunk covered with mould in spots from head to foot, but cleaned up fairly well and is now my best clo.' When he was invited by Hugh Rathbone, the Chancellor of the university from the ship-owning family, he could not find either collar studs or clothes: 'after endless search I uncovered my boots concealed in a drawer, and my clothes in a wardrobe that would not open and fell if you touched it, the top smashing on my shoulder'. The evening wasn't worth it: the food was bad; there was no alcohol; and Rathbone was uninteresting and uninterested, and rude to his wife: ' "Won't you help Dr Sampson to a little more, Hugh?"

"I have already asked Dr Sampson, dear" – severely and snubbingly.'

It was also becoming clear in the Rai's letters that his family life was breaking up behind the shaky façade. Margaret had tired of her husband's behaviour – whether his womanizing, his drinking or his temper – and was mostly living separately. The Rai insisted it was her own choice, but he probably made her life with him impossible. In term-time he stayed in his lodgings in Liverpool, while Margaret was in Wales with Honor. Often he stayed in Liverpool for the weekend, and he frequently went on holiday without the family – even at Christmas.

He continued to turn up at Bettws-Gwerfil-Goch from time to time, however. The house on the hill remained a bond between him and Margaret, with all its associations with children, friends and the open-air life. But he was concerned that his wife's more conventional friends and relations would find it primitive and Bohemian. When she wanted to invite a cousin, John Chisholm, to stay there he was appalled:

> Probably we should hear that he had said I was a man who spent all my time in the public house, that Michael was not dressed like a gentleman, and that Honor was being brought up like a pagan. And I don't want people even to *think* criticisms of our little Cae Gwyn.

He could also be absurdly pompous. In July 1916 Margaret had had a Captain Broadbent, the brother of a friend, to stay at Cae Gwyn because she wanted to talk to someone about her son Michael. The Rai was outraged that a bachelor should stay in his house in his absence, and took it as a personal insult.

Mr (or is it Captain?) Broadbent's part in this insult is a separate matter, and one simpler to deal with. As you are aware I have never met him. I know nothing of him, good or bad, and have no desire to think ill of him. I only know of him as Miss Broadbent's brother, and that he motors, and that he calls himself Uncle Tom, and that his health invites sympathy and prevents him going to the front . . .

I must ask you to let me know his address (if you are acquainted with it) in order that I may make this point at least quite clear to him. His health you tell me is not good, so I will endeavour to express myself with fitting temperance . . .

This time Margaret fought back, reminding the Rai of other respectable men such as the judge Challoner Dowdall who had stayed when her husband had been away, but promised to invite no more friends without his permission. The Rai replied still more angrily, refusing to be cast as a tyrant.

You threaten to treat me as a jailor, and to refuse to have any of your friends at the house 'without my permission'. To deprive your friends of matter for a small hymn of hate, may I explain that you have my permission now, in advance, for ever, for anyone you want, 'male or female'.

The marriage was close to breaking-point, but the real shadow that lay over Cae Gwyn was the lack of money. The Rai had always been on the verge of insolvency, as his university friends were well aware: in 1899 Walter Raleigh had tactfully offered help which predictably the Rai had refused. Later his fellow professors would praise him for 'putting luxuries before necessities' – preferring intellectual pursuits to material comforts – but that was not how it looked to Margaret. Four years after renting Cae Gwyn, he was blaming her for allowing the local tradesmen to bankrupt him:

> This thing has made me utterly ill, miserable and hopeless, unfit for work at a time when anyhow I need all my strength. I see myself again plunged in the same slough of debt and I don't like it ... What your own views are, or if you condescend to have any, I do not know.

In retaliation Margaret alluded to his expensive drinking habits and he apologized for his earlier outburst. But by 1916 she was finding the house too much, with both Michael and Amyas away, and the Rai gave notice. They found a house called Dee Side, at Llangollen – less remote than Bettws but also less in touch with authentic Romani life: 'we can boast of no deeper Gypsy than an English Lovell,' the Rai told Augustus John. Old friends were soon visiting them, beginning with 'the Rani', Mary Dowdall. But Dee Side never cast the same spell as Cae Gwyn and the Rai spent even less time there.

After three years at Llangollen the marriage finally broke up and the Sampsons decided to separate, in fact if not in law. Margaret went to her parents' house at Hunt's Cross to explain. Her mother was still fond of the Rai and was pained by the separation. Soon afterwards she died suddenly of a heart-attack, some said as a result of shock.

On moving out, the Rai took the painful decision to sell the furniture at knock-down prices, though he would have preferred to burn it 'rather than these pirates should get for nothing these things I have loved so much'. In September 1920 'a villainous looking person, who had apparently called at the University twice before, pushed his way in, and describing himself as "an officer of the law" handed me a summons.' It was the agent from Llangollen, demanding £23 in rent arrears.

Six months earlier Margaret had decided – against the Rai's advice – to go and live with her parents at Hunt's Cross to look after her aged father. Though the Rai had become reconciled to him, and despite the fact that he and Margaret were now separated, he still resented his wife's attention to her father. Money, too, was now more of a problem than ever.

> I am sending you £15 from a/c No 2. Make it go as far as possible – it will buy a lump of coal or two – for there is very little left, perhaps as much again, for an emergency. And I have no prospects, nothing to sell, no expectation of making any money in any other way.

In fact the Rai still had some paintings by Augustus John which could have been sold: 'John's star may decline,' he said with foresight, 'but these represent his early, and perhaps best, work.' He suggested that Margaret might sell the Johns and give the money to her father. 'It might be rather a pang to you, but on the other hand I don't think Michael has much interest in heirlooms.' Luckily they kept some drawings, including the sketch of the Rai.

In letters to friends the Rai would occasionally mention holidays in the English and Welsh countryside, apparently taken alone. 'I came back from a walking or rather strolling tour last Saturday,' he told Augustus in August 1919: 'My only book was a little Greek anthology.' This he translated into English verse and it was later published in the *Poetry*

Review. He also told of meeting three caravans of hawkers outside Giggleswick, who spoke quite good Romani but 'who probably gave me wrong names as they were rather suspicious'. Most holidays appeared to be linked with philological pursuits. In August 1921 he told Margaret how he walked between Settle, Appleby and Penrith, making phonetic equations with North Country speech. In the spring of 1924 he visited Conway where a mysterious young gypsy lady had told the *Liverpool Daily Post* that she had been taught 'the rudiments of ancient Greek by the witch Old Taw, and picked up Homer round the camp fire'. However, the story was, as she frankly told the Rai, a *XoXiben* (a hoax). Then he went on to Carnarvon, Pwllheli and Aberdavon, to visit an old gypsy king. His holiday plans were often vague: 'I don't quite know where I am going to,' he wrote in July 1924, 'perhaps Newtown, to begin with at any rate ... then there is Borrow's track to follow, which always gives a new side interest to any trip.' 'I may go to Wales for a few days soon,' he wrote later the same year, 'I rather hate the proximity of Xmas.'

By the time he reached the age of 60, in 1922, the Rai's letters were giving an almost consistent impression of gloom. Impending financial ruin and worsening health – gout, bronchitis, colds and aches and pains – were recurring themes. 'I am rather a broken man, financially and other ways. I must get away for a day or two,' he wrote before Christmas 1924, adding 'All good wishes for the season, which I gather is henceforward to be called Felixmass after some postcard cat.' Three years later he was complaining to the artist Lawrence Wright that 'all Trojan beverages are in my case *"streng verboten"* ' – his doctor had imposed strict limits on his drinking.

Was he really as ill and alone – even at Christmas – as

his letters suggested? And why was he quite so impoverished? His librarian's salary was better than that of many lecturers, and his university colleagues did not see him as broken or lonely. His disciples – none of them married – were still clearly hovering around him.

The Rai certainly spent much time with Dora Yates, who worked in the library and helped with the dictionary. He had often brought her to stay at Bettws or Llangollen, sometimes asking his wife to wire if she objected. With her intelligence and her Jewish family connections – she was related to both the Samuels and the Montagus – she could easily have acquired a more remunerative job. 'Dora ought to be set up with two cousins in the Cabinet,' the Rai wrote to Margaret in November 1915: 'They ought to create some well-paid post for her.' He made no attempt to conceal his closeness to Dora. When he received a thank-you letter from the gypsy parson George Hall who had been staying at Bettws he sent it on to his wife, adding, with no trace of irony, 'I hope from what he says that he doesn't think Dora was my wife.'

The second disciple, Agnes Marston or 'Kish', appeared equally loyal. Like Dora, she repeatedly travelled to and from first Bettws and then Llangollen, helping with the dictionary. She showed some promise as a librarian and the Rai found her a part-time job in the university. But Kish had never really escaped from her dominating Victorian parents: 'I think she was happiest with us and away from her appalling house,' the Rai wrote later. Then in August 1924 Kish and Dora went on holiday together near Alfoxden, Wordsworth's old village. Kish was even thinner than usual and her mouth became so dry that she could scarcely speak. The doctor diagnosed acute diabetes and shortly after Kish passed into a coma and died. Her death came as a great blow to the Rai.

The third disciple Eileen Lyster was also in and out of the library, but was becoming increasingly neurotic and of less and less use. 'Taking lessons in driving a motor-car', said the Rai, 'seems to have upset her nervous system rather badly, poor thing.' Eventually she recovered to immerse herself in Romani researches which seemed therapeutic. She spent much time with the Wood family near Liverpool, and befriended the great story-teller Betsy Wood, the great-great-granddaughter of the patriarch Abram Wood. The Rai had first discovered Betsy as a fountain of gypsy folklore, which she poured forth 'with such vividness as to thrill and astound the hearer'. Eileen published a sentimental book in 1926 called *The Gypsy Life of Betsy Wood* which the *Times Literary Supplement* said 'was more to the taste of the romantic child than to that of the serious reader'.

As for the fourth disciple, Gladys Imlach or Damaris, the Rai made no mention of her after the publication of *Freda's Fortune* in 1907. She had apparently disappeared without trace.

Nor do his letters give any clue as to whether one of the four might have been the mother of his secret child. But among his papers there is a poem in his handwriting, dated October 1915 and written in a more erotic style than anything he had ever penned to his wife:

> Loved One, what dost thou to me
> Thus to make you part of me?
> Merged in thy sweet soul I lie:
> O'er my head swims the blue sky:
> In mine ear strange melodies
> Rise and fall, and fall and rise:
> Now on floods of joy I float
> Borne in some enchanted boat,

The Missing Lover

Now I sink and now I soar –
What wave dashed me ashore?
Wave on wave, and bliss on bliss –
Is it this? Ah! is it this?
Love o'erwhelms me! I am dumb!
Hold me fast: I come! I come!

9

The Romani Bible

IN THE 1920s the gypsies continued to cast their spell over writers and artists. They were portrayed as idealized, sanitized figures by fashionable painters such as Alfred Munnings who befriended gypsies at the Epsom races, and were lavishly described by baroque writers such as Sacheverell Sitwell or Victoria Sackville-West. But with the advance of Freudian ideas gypsies were also emerging in more overtly erotic terms as dark, exciting symbols of sexual desire. In *The Virgin and the Gypsy* D. H. Lawrence told the story of a rector's daughter who encounters a handsome gypsy with a black moustache and insolent manner. He turns out to have been a brave soldier in the war, the best man with horses in the regiment. She becomes obsessed by his 'naked insinuation of desire', rejects her feeble English suitor and visits him in his caravan. When the rector's house is flooded by the swollen river, the gypsy rescues her, carrying her upstairs, laying her on the bed and warming her in his embrace. The next day he has vanished, leaving the heroine prostrate with her love for him.

The Rai in his sixties was still obsessed with gypsies erotically as well as philologically, and in 1922 he wrote a ghost story for the *Cornhill Magazine* which suggested subconscious desires. It tells how a university philologist has become friendly with a young gypsy girl called Eldorai who is convinced that he belongs to a lost gypsy tribe, the Ingrams. Eldorai insists on mixing some of his blood with hers and kneading it into dough which they both eat. Now, she says, they belong to each other, and she will come to fetch him within seven years. Two days later Eldorai falls into a quarry and dies, and the gypsy family disappears. Seven years later the philologist is amazed to hear that Eldorai has been seen in the same quarry, and is preparing to be married the next day. At midnight he revisits the quarry, where he hears Eldorai laughing happily and shouting 'this way Rai'. She takes his hand – and he dies.

The Rai was anxious to know what his friends thought of the story (Scott Macfie found it creepy). Perhaps his obsession with gypsies, his delight in their girls, his half-longing to be a gypsy himself, and his death-wish were at the root of his anxiety. In any event he refused to analyse his own motives and had little patience with the new-fangled science of psychoanalysis. When Professor Mair of the university bought books on 'psy-an' he refused to allow them on the library shelves, so that philosophy students had to borrow them from the professor's private room. Yet Margaret was interested. 'I assume', he wrote to her, 'that there may be some less appalling works, which might suit a beginner. I'd like to see the one you read, for instance, if only to do the idea justice and understand what it's really driving at. Could you lend it to me for a day or two?'

He was now more than ever established as the Rai of

Rais, as a new generation of scholars emerged to pay him respect. In 1922 the Gypsy Lore Society was relaunched in a more modest form, its Journal now issued quarterly at half of its former size and with only sparing illustrations. It was guaranteed by William Ferguson who had visited the Sampsons at Bettws and had gone camping in the caravan Esmeralda, and who now became President of the Society. Its secretary was T. W. Thompson, an expert on gypsy customs (who later also became editor), and the new Journal's first editor was E. O. Winstedt, another comparative newcomer: 'Is Winstedt a Gypsy?' Walter Raleigh asked Scott Macfie hopefully in June 1918: 'He has the shyness of the race.' At first the Rai appeared lukewarm about the relaunch: 'I don't much care really whether it is re-started or not, or who runs it,' he wrote to Margaret, 'provided it isn't Ackerley, who by the way is now a Canon!' But he was a frequent contributor.

The Rai also remained on good terms with Augustus John who had achieved a new respectability since the war, when he was commissioned to paint war leaders, amongst them the charismatic Admiral Lord ('Jacky') Fisher. 'John must now be at the top of his profession,' the Rai wrote to Margaret, 'but what I envy him most is meeting all these interesting people on the free and easy terms that obtain between artist and sitter. Fisher's conversation must have been worth listening to.' 'John has been richly dowered by his fairy godmothers,' he wrote a year later: 'Beauty, strength, friends, freedom, genius, wealth, fame, immortality. I wonder whether he is happy.'

John now moved sometimes in grander circles, staying in great houses like Chirk Castle, owned by his patron Lord Howard de Walden. When the Rai met de Walden at the university and mentioned John, he replied: ' "Oh yes, I think he left my place to go to yours" – as though Chirk

Castle and Cae Gwyn were equally famous seats.' At the same time John continued to maintain strong bonds with the Rai, corresponding copiously, and often slipping into Romani. Nostalgia featured regularly in his letters: 'Curse this London Life. I long for the open road and a good pub at the side of it,' he wrote in July 1919: 'I never cease regretting the Cymro, its landlord, his daughter and serving maid.'

The Rai for his part also kept in touch with John's family. He read a play by his sister Gwen John which had 'some of the neat clear precision of touch one used to notice in her little architectural drawings'. It was 'rather modern, and perhaps neo-Ibsenish, but queer and interesting'. Her use of the 'contemptible' dialect, however, he found exasperating: 'Why use dialect if you don't know any?' He was much more pleased to hear that one of John's sons, Henry – who went to Stonyhurst and later became a Jesuit priest – was interested in gypsy matters, unlike the other offspring of the Romani Rais. Henry became 'a most promising member' of the Gypsy Lore Society and was, according to Winstedt, 'as keen as mustard': tragically he was drowned at the age of 23 in 1930.

The Rai was now determined to finish the great dictionary of the Welsh Romani language on which he had first embarked in his prime back in 1896. Since then he had become bogged down in the morass of vocabulary. It was a common failing amongst lexicographers. James Murray, who had begun the definitive *Oxford English Dictionary* in 1888, had hopelessly underestimated 'the unknown vastness' of his work, taking three years over the letter A, while C was not published until three years after the original deadline for the whole work: the letter Z was not reached until 1928, thirteen years after Murray's death.

The Rai's own progress was limited by the lack of a written Romani literature. Though he needed no special scriptorium like Murray's to contain thousands of entries, nor armies of volunteers to sift through centuries of poetry and prose, it was nevertheless a daunting task. Over the years he filled a hundred notebooks with his recordings of gypsy phrases and words, often taken down round camp-fires, in tents or in pubs, in his own exact handwriting and notation. To establish the precise vowels and consonants he had devised a phonetic alphabet adapted from the great philologist Miklosich in which one symbol stood for one simple sound and which carefully differentiated between the sounds made by the placing of the tongue and the teeth. The sounds were analysed in the opening section of the dictionary, followed by a complete grammatical study of the language. Then in the dictionary itself he traced each word to its roots in Sanskrit, Hindi, Persian, Romanian or any of the other languages from which Romani had borrowed. It was hard work to extract precise details from the gypsies for they were, as he wrote in the preface, 'Constitutionally averse from anything that savours of drudgery, and soon reduced to a state of bewilderment by set questions . . . the Gypsy is, by common consent, the worst expositor on earth.'

The quotations demonstrating usage were taken not from writings but from conversations, folk-tales or riddles which provided their own insights into Romani life: 'What goes to London, yet stays? – The Road'; 'Is not this a disgrace? A lady to give birth to a puppy!'; 'What did she do with the darning needle? She drew blood from her own arm near the elbow, dipped her finger in the blood, and smeared it on his lips . . .'; 'The gentleman here knows the heart of the Welsh Gypsies: he reads their thoughts.'

The Rai was determined to create a fitting monument

to his beloved language which had transformed his own life. He told Augustus John it 'should prove to the judicious reader a complete guide to sorcery, fortune-telling, love and courtship, *kichimai* [inns], fiddling, harping, poaching and the life of the road generally – in fact I hope it may prove the Romani Rai's Bible'. It was not surprising that he took far longer than he had expected. The Clarendon Press were in no hurry: after postponing publication during the war they temporized further. The Rai complained bitterly in October 1919 to Margaret, with whom he still corresponded in friendly terms despite their separation:

> I have not heard yet from the Clarendon Press, and suppose they are half-ashamed to write again and explain that their answer must be for the present, in the eggbin. It is rather hard lines that after giving up the greater part of my life or its leisure to this study, after having had the amazing luck to hit upon a new and precious vein, after spending more money than I could afford and all the rest, it should be dished by the war.

When they did reply they asked him to recast the dictionary entirely on a different plan, going through the whole alphabet again: 'You may well say "courage",' he wrote to Margaret. 'It is only by not looking at the task ahead that I am able to tackle it at all. B is an appalling letter.' At last in 1925 the proofs were being sent back, and the Rai wondered whether the printing costs of £1,000 were really worth it. 'There may be three people in England who will buy a copy, but I doubt it.'

In 1926 the dictionary was finally published. 'The odd thing is that it should have appeared at all,' remarked the Rai. It was an imposing volume bound in the familiar

Oxford dark blue. Opposite the title page was the Rai's favourite quotation from George Borrow, who had dreamt of finding the gypsies of two hundred years earlier who spoke the pure Romani language: 'Supposing I had accomplished all this, what would have been the profit of it; and in what would all this wild gypsy dream have terminated?' On the next page was a dedication in Romani 'to Borrow, who for many years lit my way here, and who now smiles at me from his rainbow'.

In his preface the Rai recalled how he had first begun 'this study of an Indian language spoken in the heart of Wales', and tried to reconcile his two roles of Scholar Gypsy and Gypsy Scholar. 'An early interest in the Gypsies originating, it must be confessed, rather in a spirit of romance than of research, led me while still a boy to the acquisition of their tongue, the better to gain an inner understanding of this peculiar people.' He reminisced with nostalgia about his exotic researches into the language, but saw its vigour already fading:

My collections have been gathered in every part of Wales where members of the clan were to be found, following the Gypsy avocations of harpers, fiddlers, fishermen, horse-dealers, knife-grinders, basket-makers, wood-cutters, fortune-tellers, and hawkers ... Every Romani sentence given in the Grammar or Vocabulary is the spontaneous utterance of some Welsh Gypsy, reflecting the life and lore, customs, beliefs, thought and feeling of the race ... But while I have been fortunate in happening upon Welsh Romani in its Augustan, or at least its Silver Age, I cannot disguise from myself that decay has already begun to set in, and that another generation or two may see the end of this ancient speech.

It was an accurate prediction, as I realized two generations later when I tried to discover descendants of the
Wood clan who might still speak deep Romani, only to find
that they had abandoned the ancient speech. Yet they knew
of the dictionary, which had become their family's badge
of distinction. For the dictionary has never been super-
seded as the record of that pure language.

Back in 1926 the book was hardly a best-seller. The
Western Mail loyally proclaimed: 'ROMANI WONDER.
LIVERPOOL SCHOLAR'S GREAT DISCOVERY. THE MIRACLE.'
'Appalling, isn't it?' the Rai commented to Margaret. But
even some scholars had doubts about the dictionary's
importance. *The Times Literary Supplement* was dismissive
of this fast-dying language:

> If Romani dies, it will be dead in a sense very different
> from that in which the term is applied to Latin or to
> Greek. Lingual sterility is part of the price the gipsy pays
> for his isolation. The present volume indeed must, one
> fears, be regarded as a slightly anticipatory tombstone
> [rather] than as a guide to a living language with time
> and activity before it.

'Did you see a miserable notice', the Rai asked his wife,
'written by someone who doubts that there is such a
speech, hopes there isn't, dislikes and disapproves of
Gypsies (which he spells with a small g and an i – the test
of the rank outsider) – and hopes and believes the tongue
is dead anyway?' Margaret replied sympathetically but he
was still wounded: 'He made the mistake of *overdoing* it.
The Gypsies may be bad, may not have written an *Iliad* or
Aeneid yet, may have preserved their language merely to
evade magistrates and policemen; but still there *is* such a
language.'

Most gypsy enthusiasts, however, rallied behind the book all the more keenly because the language was so rare. As Scott Macfie said in a review:

Never has such feverish diligence been brought to the collecting of a tongue spoken by only a few score persons. There is something Gypsy-like in the contempt of material wealth that impelled a scholar to devote the best thirty years of his life to research so unremunerative, and induced the greatest university press in the world to print without hope of gain the resulting volume.

Macfie recalled his own role in 'this great book, the building of which I have watched almost from the foundation, assisting at laborious days with patient Edward Wood, comforting Taw after phonetic torture, enjoying convivial hours with Matthew'. It was a 'narrative of the Gypsies' long and leisurely walk from India to Wales'. He loved the 'piquant blend of sound science and inconsequent levity', and how the gypsies revealed themselves 'in vivid little sentences: "We are all wanderers: the dear Lord created us so." '

There was some carping from rivals. Bernard Gilliat-Smith, the expert on Balkan gypsies who had quarrelled with the Rai in 1920, was deeply offended by the lack of proper credit for his own discoveries. He began to write an acrimonious letter to the Rai but tore it up. The Rai only heard he had taken offence when told by Scott Macfie. He wrote a pained apology to Gilliat-Smith recalling his old friendship and admiration but admitting that he was sceptical about the existence of the aspirated *c* which was Gilliat-Smith's special discovery in the Balkans. He himself thought it was a combination of *t* and *s*. He had suggested

to George Grierson a gramophone experiment in a phonetician's laboratory, to play the sound backwards and see
how it came out. Gilliat-Smith replied courteously, but
insisted the aspirated *c* existed 'beyond all shadow of
doubt'. He continued to resent the Rai's scepticism long
after his death.

Most Romanophiles, however, were thrilled by the dictionary. 'Only so deep and profound a scholar,' rhap-
sodized Arthur Symons, 'only so gifted a linguist,
endowed, it seems to me, with genius, could have created
what is, essentially, and what will always remain so, this
Masterpiece.' 'It is the only dictionary I know', wrote the
architect Charles Reilly, 'which is really good reading
wherever you open it.'

Nonetheless, the Rai's achievement was less single-
handed than it appeared. In his introduction he acknowledged the help of three of his women disciples – Dora
Yates, Eileen Lyster and the late Agnes Marston (Kish) –
who 'greatly lightened my task', and he thanked Kish especially for transcribing his manuscripts. His colleagues
thought he gave them too little credit. The three women,
wrote H. J. Francis, a later secretary of the Gypsy Lore
Society, had undertaken much more than 'the collation and
arrangement of his material'. Dora had been crucial in collecting folk-tales in Welsh Romani. Without her, wrote
another later scholar R. A. R. Wade, 'the book would have
been impossible and her work in this period – insuffi-
ciently acknowledged by the Rai unfortunately – was perhaps her greatest contribution to philology *per se*'. As for
Gladys Imlach, the last disciple, she was not mentioned at
all.

10

Outcasts of Society

BY THE LATE 1920s Liverpool had lost most of the opti-
mism of its Victorian heyday, but it was still seething
with English, Welsh, Irish and Scots, with Protestants and
Catholics, each with their own giant cathedral rising from
faded terraces. It was, too, still a city of extremes, of slum-
dwellers along the river and great landowners outside the
limits, though it no longer looked to an ever-growing
future.

Liverpool University had settled into a more respectable
and conventional middle age under the moral philosopher
Hector Hetherington, who became vice-chancellor in 1927.
Hetherington evidently expressed some concern about the
Rai's Bohemian habits, and there was gossip among the
students about his past amorous pursuits: one of them
recorded a story of him being discovered with a woman
student in the council room, on the table. But in the library
the Rai was a local institution, feared and admired by most
of his assistants. Librarianship was still emerging as a new

John Sampson at the age of 65, by Lawrence Wright

and uncertain profession: the Rai, said his successor
Garmon Jones, had made it 'fit for a scholar and a gentleman'. 'Few who came into contact with him are likely to
forget him,' wrote his assistant Lionel Bradley:

> That massive dome of a head, more memorable than St
> Peter's or St Paul's, tilted a little forward; the eyes peer-
> ing quizzically through the gold-rimmed glasses, the
> slow, courteous, expectant smile. Was it the smile of a
> tiger about to pounce?

As the Rai approached the retirement age of 65 in November 1927 the chairman of the Council, Hugh Rathbone, urged
a year's delay, explaining that Dr Sampson was a great
scholar famous all over the world. The Rai welcomed the
postponement of poverty, but commented to Margaret: 'I
wish great scholars were better paid. Not a halfpenny from
the Clarendon Press for my book!' When the Rathbones
invited him to a reception, he felt he could not face it – he
had gout in his ankle.

The following year, as retirement loomed, a group of
friends including Scott Macfie, Augustus John and Robert
Bridges organized a 'Sampson Fund' to tide him over. The
many contributors ranged from Oliver Lodge and Edwin
Lutyens to the three women disciples and the gypsy Jim
Wade, who sent 2s 6d. By October 1928 the Rai was facing
'the awesome shadow of the formal farewell'. He wanted,
perhaps with a twinge of guilt, to give Margaret a present
'out of the spoil, if any'.

The valedictory dinner was held at the University Club.
Professor Campagnac of the education department gave a
moving extempore speech, praising the Rai's 'serene and
magnificent detachment' from other men's ambitions –
advancement, success, money, fame – and holding him up

as an example of one who set the things of ultimate worth before those of mean and immediate utility. The Rai in turn looked back on his thirty-six years – reflecting on how conditions had changed since he had first begun and praising his successor Garmon Jones.

Retirement did not come easily. He told Macfie that he 'had on the whole a glorious share of life' and saw no reason why his 'last years should not be years of pleasantness and peace'. But he realized that the tearing up of old roots would be a shock, for he was, as Macfie wrote, leaving a library where every volume was a personal friend.

He began to hate Liverpool and told Margaret he felt he had to get away from his university colleagues 'from a sense of decency which made one abhor the thought of barging into them continually, with futile questions and answers'.

He thought about Wales and spent an emotional weekend at Bettws with old friends – 'we seem to have become part of history' – but it was too far to visit regularly. Then he found rooms in Shrewsbury, which had some gypsies nearby and was close to Wales, in a house called West Hermitage, 'for which I hope my mind will be quiet and religious enough to suit'. It had a cheerful landlady and two other 'harmless' lodgers. The house was less romantic than it sounded, but he loved the surrounding countryside: 'The river winds so much that Shrewsbury is almost an island . . . One could hardly be dull in such a lovely old place.'

'It's rather amazing how entirely I have forgotten the Library now,' he wrote to Garmon Jones, his only real friend left at the university, who understood his sensitivities:

It seems to have vanished like a dream – or nightmare! Yet I suppose the same old seasons and duties recur.

Who now – can it be thou O Garmon? – adjusteth his features in a congealed smile and hasteneth to meet and greet the Members and Memberesses of the Workers' Educational Guild and – once more – displayeth for their delectation the Cartoons of Raphael and M. Angelo . . .

Now that he was no longer circumscribed by the university, the gypsies beckoned more forcefully. Wild wandering gypsies were increasingly hard to find, as cars, local councils and urban sprawl encroached on their way of life, but the Rai still tracked them down. He told Augustus John of a visit to Wales 'where I have been gypsy-ing with the usual success! I chased Charley Wood from Dolgelley to Dyffrun and thence to Portmadoc only to find he had just departed for Cheshire.' Later he met

> some perfect Gypsies of the untamed order on the road to Boyston Hill. Young man, with pointed ringlets round his face and still wilder young wife who suckled her naked child unabashed in the Compasses, whither I led them, while their host of young children swarmed around the room.

He began to compile an anthology about the 'different value of life to the gypsy and gentile stock'. In this he had been partly inspired by a remark made by his young gypsy friend Rosie Griffiths. He had told her about Wordsworth's poem on gypsies which ends

> . . . they are what their birth
> And breeding suffer them to be;
> Wild outcasts of society.

'Are you aware', the Rai had asked Rosie, 'that

Wordsworth, the great Mr Wordsworth, has called you a
"wild outcast of Society"?' And Rosie had replied dis-
dainfully: 'There are two societies.' This duality was the
theme of the anthology, whose title he took from Borrow:
The Wind on the Heath. As he wrote in the preface,

> Yes, certainly there are two Societies, and which is the
> happier remains a question. Do we not find Shakespeare
> – through the mouth of Amiens – Hazlitt, Kinglake,
> Stevenson, Housman, Masefield, and many another –
> sometimes wondering whether Madam Civilization may
> not have put her money on the wrong horse?

The book was commissioned by C. H. Prentice of Chatto
& Windus, with whom the Rai struck up a friendly correspondence, and Augustus John came up with another
frontispiece – his painting *A Gitana's Head,* owned by his
lover Mrs Valentine Fleming. The selection was very
personal, summing up the gypsy influences on the
Rai's life. George Borrow still predominated, and most
of the Rai's friends were there, including the earlier
scholar gypsy Francis Hindes Groome, Charles Leland the
American philologist, Theodore Watts-Dunton and his
friend Algernon Swinburne, Arthur Symons the forlorn
poet, and Augustus John. The passages selected all vindi-
cated the gypsy lifestyle, beginning with Cervantes' fine
eulogy from 'La Gitanilla de Madrid' written in 1614:

> We are the Lords of the Universe, of fields, fruits, crops,
> forests, mountains, of the rivers and springs, of the stars
> and all the elements. Having learned early to suffer, we
> suffer not at all. We sleep as calmly and easily on the
> ground as on the softest bed, and our hard skin is an
> impregnable armour against the assaults of the air.

And the anthology ended with lines from George Borrow – Mr Petulengro's opinion of life and death from *Lavengro*: 'There's the wind on the heath, brother; if I could only feel that, I would gladly live for ever.'

The book was published in 1930 and was quite well reviewed. Vita Sackville-West (whom the Rai had quoted in the anthology) was enthusiastic on the radio: it was a book for every lover of the open air and Nature. But Edmund Blunden in *The Nation*, the Rai grumbled, was 'too interested in himself to be specially warm . . . did you ever hear such an unfortunate collocation of names as Edmund Blunden! His mother must be stone deaf to the poetry of sound at any rate.'

The Rai also began to explore his own Cornish roots. After his penurious childhood he was all the keener to trace his prosperous Sampson ancestors who had been engineers and small landowners in Cornwall, based at Gwennap near Falmouth where the churchyard is still full of Sampsons. He immersed himself in parish registers and eventually assembled an intricate genealogy which he had printed for the family.

To his surprise his pursuit stimulated interest in his own offspring: 'Is this one of the signs of old age?' But he was more concerned about their names and their forebears than them themselves. When I was born in 1926 he was glad that 'our branch of the family is to be continued in the male line', but he emphasized the importance of 'starting off a boy (or girl) with a good praenomen. Is "Anthony" named yet? Seward would be a good second name, if it were not for the unfortunate initials.' The problem was solved by adding Terrell, a family name.

When my brother John was born the Rai calculated that he could have been conceived in Cornwall, so he 'should be a true Cornubian'. He wanted him to be called Edmond after a 'direct ancestor ten generations earlier', but did not wish to appoint himself 'Nomenclator-in-Chief to the Sampson Clan' and could hardly object to John. Instead he sent a Christmas present of folk-tale nursery rhymes for his mother to chant to him.

When Honor became engaged to Jack Matthew, an eligible solicitor from Cambridge, his chief curiosity was whether his family was originally Cornish or Welsh – 'There are Cornish families with both one and two t's.'

He wrote only sporadically to his two surviving children and to his wife, usually with news of ill-health. At the age of 68 he told Margaret:

> I used to think sometimes that I should be fortunate if I reached my father's age – 59. And now I wonder whether I have been so fortunate. Well I suppose I shall think myself fairly fortunate if tonight is better than last night, or the one before that, but I don't mean to speak of my ailments. Roughly gout and rheumatism and bronchitis.

After a year at Shrewsbury his landlady began to make plans to sell the house so he had to move once more. He thought of going south but in the end decided to move much closer to Liverpool, to the suburban seaside resort of West Kirby on the Wirral peninsula across the Mersey which his doctor thought might alleviate his bronchitis. It was a curious decision in the light of his earlier desire to avoid Liverpool at all costs. His rooms were in a mock-Tudor house near the sea, in Brookfield Gardens. As he told a friend:

> A useful mnemonic aid to Brookfield is BF with which initials you can, if you please, associate your old friend
>
> John Sampson

Once ensconced in West Kirby he was soon grumbling to Margaret again: 'Even in May the weather keeps cheerless and bleak: my only comfort is that it would be worse at Shrewsbury.' Yet he seemed friendlier towards her, and she even came up to Liverpool in June 1930 to join him in staying with Garmon Jones. All the same, she appeared to know nothing of his social life in West Kirby, or of who looked after him, and he did not enlighten her.

By November 1930 he was telling Augustus John that he might move again. 'Of course this *vlija* bores me to death . . . I might settle in Oxford, if it were not for the cultured crew which one stumbles against at every step . . . My sympathies have swung back to the "other society".' John proposed Salisbury, near his own house at Fordingbridge. But the Rai stuck it out in the north: 'I hardly see anyone . . . planted here like a potato.'

The gypsy dream still kept him going. He felt a strong urge, he told John, to finish off his 'old stuff' including Shelta, folk-tales and Romani poetry. He collected some Welsh folk-tales for the Gregynog Press which published limited editions. And the Oxford University Press agreed to publish his poems in Romani which he had written and collected together twenty years before. He again asked John for a frontispiece and the artist was as generous as ever: 'Of course I'd be sad to miss being in this book, for our friendship has meant a very great deal to me and our gypsying together one of the major episodes in my blooming life.' He duly sent six drawings of a gypsy courtship which became 'more and more indecorous'. And he added: 'I think perhaps the big girl with a chap gazing at her and *not* mauling her about would do best.' The Rai took his advice. The picture showed a bosomy half-naked gypsy girl being watched by a gypsy boy and it formed the frontispiece to the book which was entitled *Romane Gilia, John Sampsoneste.*

After his sixty-ninth birthday the Rai sounded cheerful enough in a letter to my father: 'I have just edited an East Anglian Romani Vocab. of 1798, which came my way by the merest chance.' To his wife he painted a different picture: 'How to write prettily about one's health is an art I have never mastered . . . Of course I have bronchitis, complicated by tonsilitis and glands, and my nights are pretty trying.'

In July he came to stay with my parents in our house in Hampstead for Honor's wedding. He made a fuss about the party, refusing to wear spats but agreeing to a frock coat. 'Is there any one *special* who is coming to the great ceremony?' he asked Margaret: 'I shall naturally be the least important person there, the cynosure of *no* eye.' My mother was apprehensive about this uneasy reunion but we children were excited about meeting our father's father. He turned out to be a charming old man: he put my sister Dorothy on his knee and showed her how to make cat's cradles. It was clear that he came from another universe.

He enjoyed the family occasion, and the visit south: Augustus John found him 'genial and youthful in spirit and as clear-minded as ever'. He went back north apparently content and active, and expected to be off soon for a short holiday in Wales. He was delighted that Honor had just visited Bettws: 'It must have been rather like a Royal Progress! The joy and excitement!' He would send a book of gypsy folk-tales to Dorothy, and Margaret his gypsy poems for her opinion. A week later he was very lame with gout or rheumatism, 'I suppose I must lump it.'

A week after that he wrote to Margaret with unusual warmth, as if something had suddenly changed. For the first time he suggested she visit West Kirby: 'Couldn't you try it if only for once? I should welcome a visit, and like you to see my room, and books, and bits of things picked up here and there.'

That was the last news. He died a month later, in the early morning of 9 November 1931, with no member of the family present. His death marked the end of one story, but was the prelude to another.

11

Funeral and Fury

IT WAS ONLY after my grandfather died that my grand-mother and her two surviving children were confronted with the extent of his alternative life. The first and most embarrassing clue lay in his choice of executors: his fellow expert on gypsies, Scott Macfie, and Dora Yates. It was Dora, now a determined and dedicated scholar in her late forties, who emerged, to my family's distress, as the chief guardian of the Rai's inheritance and reputation.

My grandmother was hurt and humiliated to discover that the man she had loved and cared for had virtually dis-owned her. Whatever she had known, or not wanted to know, about the Rai's adultery, she was now publicly cast as the wronged and discarded wife. Dora, not Margaret, had been with him over the weekend before he died when a specialist had inspected his painful throat and found a cancer. 'The Rai was perfectly happy on the Saturday and Sunday, and had been working as usual,' Dora told Macfie. 'When I left his house about 9.30 pm his last words were

"Won't it be fun if my *Romane Gilia* are out by the time you come next Friday?" ' He died alone and painlessly from heart failure at about 3 o'clock on Monday morning, when he was rising from his bed to get a book.

Dora had a terrible time coping with the lawyers and planning the cremation by herself, until she was joined on the Monday evening by the Rai's legitimate family – his widow Margaret, his son Michael and his daughter Honor with her husband Jack Matthew who was chosen as the executors' solicitor. The family had to make arrangements together with Dora, which soon generated tension about the gypsy funeral – the Rai had decreed that it should be held on the mountain Foel Goch near his beloved village of Bettws-Gwerfil-Goch.

The Rai remained a pagan to the end and stipulated that 'my death shall be attended by no religious ceremony of any kind whatsoever'. He may have had occasional doubts. He had once jokingly described his death-bed scene to his friend Glyn Davies:

Eh? What? The Devil! Half an hour to live and repent of an ill spent life and go to glory. No time for philosophic doubts now. Fetch the bishop in his motor car, mobilize the curates, beat the big drum, strike up 'the blood of the lamb'. Yes, I believe! Yes, I repent! Any more formulae or creeds? Yes, I accept them all! Eh? Burn my Romany grammar, and poems? Certainly! Sell my rare books and give the proceeds to the Bible Society? With pleasure!

But in his last years he was set on a heathen memorial, to the distress of his family. 'I can see they will evade the Foel Goch ceremony if they can,' Dora complained bitterly to Macfie. 'They wanted a nice pretty funeral, and were furious at not being allowed to do this.'

After the cremation Dora was left alone to sort out and pack up the Rai's belongings with the help of Rosie Griffiths, the gypsy from the Wood tribe who had been with him before he died. That evening Dora and Rosie took his most intimate possessions including his false teeth and threw them into a nearby lake: 'true Gypsy fashion, and what he would have desired'.

The plans for the funeral were a still fiercer source of resentment for Margaret. Dora went to great pains to organize it as the Rai would have wished: he wanted no official university representatives, only friends and gypsies. She arranged for the harpist Reuben Roberts, who had married Rosie Griffiths' sister Mary-Lizzie, to come to play music, though 'that old scoundrel' insisted on a fee in advance. Margaret Sampson then demanded that there should be no women present (presumably dreading a parade of the Rai's old girlfriends), which meant excluding Romani notables such as Esmeralda Lock, Alabaina Robinson and Lureni Boswell; but Dora herself, as executrix, could not be kept away.

To the Romanophiles the Rai's death came as a double bereavement for it marked the fading of their gypsy dream as well as the end of a friend. 'It's a ghastly blow to me, for the Rai was so much part of my life,' Augustus John told Margaret. In a more expansive letter to Dora, he wrote, 'I was on the point of writing to him and hoped soon to foregather with him again as of old over the *Gilia* and a glass in some pleasant *Kirčuma*.' In *The Times* Oliver Elton described him as 'a man on a large scale, both mentally and physically ... A wanderer in the open, he brought a breath of the "wind on the heath" into the professorworld.' With more candour Scott Macfie wrote to my father: 'There is nobody I have quarrelled with more often and nobody whose loss I feel more.'

Macfie prepared a long and candid obituary for the Gypsy Lore Society's Journal under his pen-name Andreas. The Rai, he wrote, disliked jokes against himself: after Macfie had pulled his leg he had stayed in a huff for months until the gypsies reconciled them. He had an uncontrollable temper and once threw whisky into a colleague's face. He resented colleagues who made discoveries he envied. In middle age 'his modest bearing stiffened until it was well nigh pontifical ... he appeared self-assertive and overbearing, difficult of approach, almost tyrannical'. But Macfie concluded: 'The Rai had a thousand faults and I love him for every one of them.'

The Rai's will, which he had revised three years before, came as another shock to his family, for it divided the two sides of his life, and showed clearly which side he preferred. He left Dora all his papers and letters, asking that she should prepare some for publication, while leaving all his Romani books to the Gypsy Lore Society. To Augustus John he bequeathed his Smith & Wesson revolver No. 239892 'as a small memento of long friendship'. (When the *Evening News* asked John for an explanation for this strange bequest he replied, 'It's nobody's business but my own.') On the other side he left his daughter Honor £1,000, and his two grandchildren at the time of the will – myself and my sister Dorothy – £100 each, which never seemed to arrive. He bequeathed anything left over, and there was very little, to his widow.

Scott Macfie was in poor health, so Dora took sole charge of the funeral arrangements. Immediately after the Rai's death gypsies began sending messages to her in Liverpool insisting that they attend the ceremony. Just after the cremation Ithal Lee arrived at Dora's house having walked ten miles, explaining that he had promised the Rai he would scatter his ashes and asking why the Rai's son had not yet arranged the ceremony. My father, who was about to sail for Shanghai, wanted to postpone it, but Macfie and Dora were firm about the urgency of the matter. 'I feel rather strongly that Miss Yates is morally bound to carry out some such ceremony and that I have failed in a trust,' Macfie told him sternly. 'Your father intended it so to be, and as his only expressed wish, I think it ought to be done as an act of piety – but with reverence.'

On 17 November an advertisement appeared in the *Liverpool Echo:*

To Gypsies

DR JOHN SAMPSON'S ASHES will be scattered upon Foel Goch, Llangwm, near Corwen, on Saturday next, the 21st instant, at 12.30 p.m. All Gypsies in the neighbourhood who desire to be present should assemble with fiddles and harps at the Inn, Llangwm, at 12 noon.

On the morning of 21 November a motor-coach of mourners set off from Liverpool for Wales, my father, Dora and an odd mixture of professors and gypsies among them. Augustus John had driven up from London with his sculptor friend Stephen Tomlin, while Scott Macfie had painfully travelled down from the Pennines. They arrived at the small village of Llangwm, just below the mountain of Foel Goch, to find a crowd of hundreds already waiting, including a large contingent from Bettws and a group of journalists, among them British Movietone News, who had got wind of an event. Dora professed to be distressed by the presence of the press – 'I am afraid the publicity was unavoidable,' she apologized to John afterwards – and

Macfie too was worried. But the reporters entered into the spirit of the occasion and their stories were respectful.

The straggling crowd was marshalled by Macfie and my father to walk slowly up the mountain, led by Ithal Lee and Manfri, the son of Matthew Wood, and followed by other gypsies including Matthew's three other sons Turpin, Jim and Howell, and the musicians. Then walked my father, John, and Macfie on a pony, followed by professors and other Liverpool friends. Some mourners struggled out of breath up the steep slope, but Macfie thought the procession 'not undignified'. Below the mountain top, looking across to Snowdonia, John proclaimed the oration and my father scattered the ashes. He was clearly under strain among these strange fellow-mourners. John thought he wore an expression 'of some disdain' while the *Daily Express* described him as having 'a set, expressionless face'. But to Dora he seemed splendid, startling many of the gypsies by his resemblance to the Rai. She was especially moved by the mysterious white cloud which floated up from the Rai's ashes: 'it made me feel that truly he was now "Rolled round in earth's diurnal course, With rocks and stones and trees."' The mourners recited the Romani farewell and Reuben Roberts played on the triple harp, though Ithal poured scorn on his playing and the Woods and the Griffiths complained about his leadership.

Then the mourners walked slowly down the mountain to Llangwm. Dora succeeded in steadying herself with the help of the gypsies: 'I couldn't show the University set that I cared too much.' They all reassembled for the funeral feast at Cerig-y-Drudion, where George Borrow had once stayed and which the Owen family had owned for eleven generations. Philology mingled with festivity. Rosie Griffiths talked gaily throughout the meal in Welsh, English or Romani. When John complained that a phrase was too 'deep' for him, she teased him: *'Dikh andray i bore Reske lilesti* [Look in the great Rai's book].' Turpin Wood boasted to John that only he knew the gypsy word *tautoleero*, carrion crow, which could be found in the Rai's book, and explained it was so named 'because it *tears* its prey'. 'Nothing would have pleased the Rai better', the gypsy expert John Myers commented afterwards, 'than that such an addition should have been made at his funeral feast.' '*Wouldn't* the Master have been pleased', Dora wrote to John later, 'with the scene in that oak-beamed kitchen?' He was not quite so sure, as he subsequently recalled: 'I thought this celebration lacked spontaneity.'

The Rai was more famous dead than he had ever been alive, at least for a day. The popular press as well as *The Times* and the *Daily Telegraph* relished the bizarre mixture of gypsies and professors amongst the mourners. The *Daily Express* even began its story – those were the days! – with a quotation from Robert Browning's 'The Grammarian's Funeral':

> Here's the top-peak; the multitude below
>   Live, for they can, there:
> This man decided not to Live but Know –
>   Bury this man there?
> Here – here's his place, where meteors shoot, clouds
>   form,
>   Lightnings are loosened,
> Stars come and go! let joy break with the storm,
>   Peace let the dew send!
> Lofty designs must close in like effects:
>   Loftily lying,
> Leave him – still loftier than the world suspects,
>   Living and dying.

After the funeral many gypsies wrote to Dora to express their grief in letters all the more moving for their misspellings and uncertain hands. These she filed away in the library. Turpin Wood wrote from The Hand at Bettws-Gwerfil-Goch, thanking Dora for a photograph of Dr Sampson which he had already had framed, and enclosing photos of his children – Violet May, Jim Turpin and Robert John – at the Rai's funeral. 'And you may rest assured that I speak ROMANY to them. Mr Huth and my cousin Rosy called this summer and we had quite a nice time in the Hand.' An unnamed gypsy from Llanrwst wrote a letter to 'Dear Sister and Brothers', which was passed on to Dora.

Well I suppose you know that Sampson is Dead and was buried Wednesday, seeing the photo in the paper. It was in Shrewsbury we seen him last. It was a great shock and I wonder as anybody been to your house since he died . . . I mean such as Dora. As you know she was allways with him. He was stay-in in West Kirby, and I suppose that's where he was buried, and that's that . . . Well you know that the Ry has been a good gentleman . . .

For the Rai's friends the mountain ceremony remained a memorial both to their hero and to their own lost youth. The scattered ashes, the wailing music and the burnt-out box summed up the lure of the open air and the rejection of material values. Augustus John, Dora and Scott Macfie would talk and write about it for the rest of their lives. But for my father, though he was himself a lifelong atheist, the pagan funeral remained a traumatic realization of the gulf which had separated father from son.

Dora was clearly to be the chief guardian not only of the Rai's papers but also of his memory and reputation, and to the exclusion of his family. She was now a Romani scholar in her own right, and as executrix she made the most of it, appropriating all the Rai's papers with a possessiveness which exasperated the family. She was properly impressed by my father's moral rectitude. 'He is a fine man,' she told Macfie 'and the most truthful person I have ever met in my life.' But the Rai had warned her that Michael undervalued things of sentimental family interest; and while he was in China on business she hung on to all the Sampson family papers, thus provoking an angry correspondence with my grandmother. When my father returned from China he politely asked Dora to give them back, but Macfie recommended that Dora point out some facts which 'may not be altogether pleasant for Michael to read', including the fact, which I find poignant, that the Rai had told Dora 'that he wanted the papers kept carefully for Michael's sons (whether or not they seem interesting to Michael) . . . what is not particularly interesting to generation n is eagerly sought for by generation $n + 1$ . . . On receiving an assurance that he will not part with them except to his sons when they are old enough, you will be pleased to hand them over to Michael.'

Eventually the papers were returned to Michael, but Dora and Macfie were still keeping some secrets back. 'I don't think I ever advised telling him about Mrs Sampson's letters,' Macfie wrote to Dora, 'though I would probably do it myself if he came here. It will depend on his attitude to his aunt whom I take to be a mischievous old cat.' Exactly what my great-aunt Alice had told my grandmother ('Mater') does not emerge, but three months later my mother told my father: 'Apparently Aunt Alice has some great secret which she told to Mater but made her promise not to pass on!'

What is clear from the letters, all neatly filed in Liverpool, is that while my father was in Shanghai his mother's full fury had erupted against Dora. Immediately after the Rai's death Margaret had gone up to West Kirby and had raved to Dora about the 'wicked will' and delivered a diatribe against the Rai's 'notorious infidelity to many women'. Dora had tried to conciliate her, asking her to the funeral to 'take her rightful place and lead us' but she would not. In due course she calmed down, saying that Dora had 'always been my friend, and still was'. But after the funeral Dora was taken aback by Margaret's bitterness, for she had been generous to Margaret in the past. She had, she told Macfie, agreed to pay half the rent for the cottage at Bettws and had settled all Margaret's debts before she left Liverpool, so that Dora had had to go without new clothes for two years.

Macfie too received long tirades from Margaret, 'full of the pent-up bitterness of twenty years', which distressed him because he was fond of her. He had hoped to act as a buffer between Dora and Margaret, to take blows from both sides; but he did not know the full truth about the Rai's lovers, as Dora had to warn him:

I don't want you to jump into the ring as Mrs S's champion without knowing the full *taciben* [truth] – which she does. All the difficulties have arisen through *lako juniben trusal vaver komono* [knowledge about another person], whose interests I must protect, and if you act (blindly, in a way) for her, I may be betraying my trust and not doing what the Rai meant me to do.

Dora was worried that the 'sneering world' would gossip about the Rai's philandering and thought that 'half the folks at the Liverpool University now are very vile': the *Daily Post* had published an 'atrocious' article on the day of the funeral. She was worried too about the publication in December of the Rai's youthful Romani poems about seductive gypsy girls and his 'Five Wives', which might be taken as 'autobiographic truth'. 'I dread the *Daily Post* review . . . it is sure to be offensive and personal.'

Margaret, too, was threatening to stir up trouble at the university. In February the following year she wrote Dora a long and 'spiteful' letter blaming her for the separation and complaining that she, Margaret, was depicted as 'the unloving wife of a faithful husband'. She accused Dora of reviving gossip by her advertisements to gypsies about the funeral and demanded that she publicly apologize.

Macfie sympathized with Margaret's unhappiness, for she had always loved the Rai: 'she suffered agony secretly for years', he told Dora, 'in order that the Rai might keep his position in the University and continue his work'. Margaret might, he thought, be reproaching herself for having rejected the Rai's late attempt at reconciliation. He could not believe that Margaret was ever blamed for the separation, for although he did not know all about her husband's lovers 'I do know that the Rai's polygamy has been the subject of talk for many years'.

12

The Last Romantic

THE MAINSTAY OF the Romanophiles was now Dora Yates who was determined to perpetuate the Rai's memory. Soon she was immersed in editing his papers while effectively running the Gypsy Lore Society. A selection of the Rai's occasional verse and prose, chosen and introduced by her (she omitted the bawdier poems), was published by the Liverpool University Press under the title *In Lighter Moments*. But she complained to Augustus John that the volume was not selling and implored him to give away copies: 'I should so like to prove to our benighted University Press that John Sampson is still remembered outside sordid old Liverpool.'

Dora leant heavily on Scott Macfie who supervised the Journal while leaving Dora to handle the spade-work. Macfie, like Sampson, was a stickler for accuracy and was occasionally shocked by Dora's sentimentality and lack of rigour towards contributors. He once rudely told her, as she herself recalled,

I sometimes think that you have some of the worst qualifications possible for editorship: impetuosity, partiality
for the writer rather than his written word, and a dislike of the drudgery of checking other members' references, though I must admit that Sampson's work has
implanted in you a certain degree of accuracy.

Macfie gave Dora 'the most intensive and gruelling
training of my life'. Never a feminist, though she could
herself be bossy, she enjoyed a dominating boss like the
Rai. 'I should have been pure "school-marm" myself, if the
Rai had not saved me early in my life,' she admitted to
Macfie. 'The Rai used to say I was apt to get "uppish" if
not snubbed occasionally – and oh! how I miss that chaff
and criticism.' She relished her visits to Macfie at
Wensleydale, surrounded by exotic local characters, and
was delighted when he explained: 'All my friends are
poachers.'

When Macfie died in 1935 she almost literally stepped
into his shoes, buying his bungalow at Shaws, and later
his gypsy caravan and horse. From there she continued to
run the Gypsy Lore Society without either typewriter or
secretarial assistance. She also arranged for Liverpool
University to buy Macfie's unique collection of gypsy
books and then became its curator. She now virtually *was*
the Society.

By the 1930s the gypsies in Britain were more fashionable
and respectable, though also more idealized. Lady Eleanor
Smith, the daughter of Lord Birkenhead, had come under
the gypsies' spell through reading Borrow as a child. At
the age of 18 she was launched into society as the senior
débutante when her father was Lord Chancellor, but she
soon rebelled by going off with a circus and writing a

novel, *The Tent of Shem*. This was followed by *The Red Wagon* which became a best-seller. Like so many Romanophiles Lady Eleanor insisted that she had inherited gypsy blood through her great-grandmother Bathsheba. Her brother and biographer, the second Lord Birkenhead, was exasperated that Eleanor should see the gypsies 'through the eyes of Borrow, romanticized, a race apart, shorn of squalor and rascality, an hallucination that survived repeated contacts with them'. He was especially upset because her claim to gypsy blood was spread abroad by others, including Winston Churchill in his book *Great Contemporaries*. Indeed it was this book which persuaded the Nazis in Germany to schedule the whole family for extermination because of their impurity of blood.

A new generation of Romani enthusiasts were now moving into the Gypsy Lore Society, among them Walter Starkie who had published his book *Raggle Taggle* about gypsies in Hungary and Romania in 1933. Starkie had first discovered gypsies when he had been at Shrewsbury School where he encountered Zekie Lock, one of the true-born gypsy Shropshire clan. And it was Lock who first told him about John Sampson, the Rai from Liverpool 'who wandered about the countryside following the Gypsy trail with two *tarni rawnies* [Dora and Kish] who he took with him to the Gypsy camps ...'

In 1938 the Gypsy Lore Society celebrated its fiftieth anniversary, and Dora planned a great Jubilee dinner. Lady Arthur Grosvenor, who had loyally championed the gypsies on Epsom Downs every Derby Day, presided regally. Bernard Gilliat-Smith came over from Sofia where he was still British Consul. Walter Starkie, now a professor at Trinity College, Dublin, also came. Lady Eleanor Smith arrived by aeroplane just in time. Amongst the guests there were comparative newcomers including George Walton from the British Embassy in Moscow and Patrick McEvoy, who had just published *The Gorse and the Briar*. There were also gypsies from the old days: Rosie Griffiths, Ithal Lee who greeted guests with his wife Annie, and Harry Wood who played his 'devil's tune' on the fiddle after dinner. Augustus John, now President of the Society, sent a telegram regretting his absence but added 'it would be better and happier for you if the lovely Eleanor Smith were to sit in my seat'. The guests sat down to a gypsy meal with the menu in Romani, and Walter Starkie proposed the toast of the Society. 'He felt and made us all feel', said another member, 'that the spirit of the great John Sampson was with us that night.'

It was the last great celebration of the Romanophiles. A year later, the Second World War cast its dark shadow over the gypsy enchantment. Conscription, ration-books and wartime controls restricted the travellers still further. Some romantics hoped that new hardships would induce the gypsies to return to their natural lifestyle after a period of relative prosperity. In 1944, in *Gypsies of Britain*, Brian Vesey-Fitzgerald explained how 'Modern conditions, industrialisation and the sixpenny bazaar have destroyed that prosperity, have reduced the Gypsies again to poverty, and at the same time have saved them. There cannot be the slightest doubt that tents and ponies, not living-wagons and the team of piebalds, are the true possessions of the Gypsies.' It was not to be.

The Gypsy Lore Society survived on Dora's dedication. Though she had retired from the university library she was now an authority in her own right, with a flair for publicity. In 1948 Phoenix House published her *Gypsy Folk Tales*, illustrated by John's portrait of the gypsy Athaliah. Dora also tried to record members of the Wood family speaking Romani for the BBC, but it was too late. As she told

Augustus John in January 1952, Rosie Griffiths had lost her voice after being treated with radium; her brothers could still speak 'the deep tongue' but one was stone deaf and the other could not be found; Manfri Wood could only speak a few words and none of the younger generation could '*raker Romanes*'. Deep Romani was becoming a dead language.

At Liverpool Dora was depressed by the academic bureaucracy trampling over the 'great Sampsonian tradition' and needed John to rescue her from the 'gulf of dark despair'. She began writing her autobiography which she kept secret from my side of the family. 'I DON'T want any of the Sampsons to know that I have written down these memories until – if ever – the book appears in print,' she told her protégée Mary Arnold. But she was interested to hear news from Mary of Michael Sampson's unpromising sons. In June 1951 I had just arrived in South Africa to join the magazine *DRUM* which had been started by my Oxford friend Jim Bailey, the son of the gold millionaire Sir Abe Bailey. 'Thank you for telling me about Michael's family,' Dora wrote to Mary: 'I am truly grieved that he should be so troubled by Anthony and John's affairs, but trust that both their careers will turn out better in the future than Michael now expects – though a paper run by Abe Bailey sounds depressing in the extreme.'

Dora's autobiography, *My Gypsy Days*, was published by Phoenix in 1953. She was by now so distant from the Sampson family that I heard nothing of it until nearly forty years later – to my regret, for it is a delightful account of her life-long devotion to the gypsies and the Rai, though she never came clean about their relationship. She ended by championing her romanticism 'in this mechanised regimented world':

I shall be accused of using the 'romantic approach' in describing my Gypsies. But my reply is that Gypsies *are* romantic: 'the last romance', as Arthur Symons said, 'left in the world'. . . .

Some of us are born utilitarians and some are born romantics.

Dora still kept the Rai's memory alive. The next year she organized a BBC radio discussion with Augustus John and Manfri Wood at The White Lion at Bala, ostensibly about gypsies but mostly about the Rai. John, sounding drunk, yearned for the open road. Manfri falteringly sang a gypsy song and reminisced about the great funeral. BBC television also featured Manfri in a programme from North Wales which harked back to the Rai's days at Bettws-Gwerfil-Goch. 'Perhaps there is just time', wrote Maurice Wiggin in the *Sunday Times*, 'for some genius to make a great true film of Gypsy life, before it vanishes.'

No such genius appeared and the open road was now hemmed in by new legislation, fussy local councils and fenced-off land. The post-war 'Gypsy problem' was ably analysed in 1953 by a young recruit to the Society, Angus Fraser, a civil servant who helped Dora with the editing of the Journal and who would later become Permanent Secretary of Customs and Excise, and special adviser to Mrs Thatcher on efficiency in government. Fraser described how the Public Health Act of 1936 and the Town and Country Planning Act of 1947 were threatening the free movement of the wayfarers.

They must not spend the night on the grass verge of the road. They may generally stay for twenty-four or forty-eight hours, as the case may be, on common land if they are fortunate enough to find it.

It was a long way from Borrow's 'wind on the heath'. The new generation of Romanophiles were rightly more concerned about the political rights and social conditions of the gypsies than had been the romantic philologists. A few effective campaigners, like the Labour MP Norman Dodds and the journalist C. H. Rolph, publicized their grievances, but the bureaucracy of the welfare state was at odds with the genuinely nomadic gypsies. As Fraser put it:

Modern civilisation, of course, was not designed for such people, who are essentially a very small minority. One can understand – but hardly approve – the tendency to regard them as a social anachronism and the meticulous desire to make them live like other people. They throw the machinery of administration out of gear. Is this machinery adaptable enough to allow the Gypsies to survive, or will they be crushed into abandoning their traditional way of life?

There were still some eccentric recruits among gypsy enthusiasts. In 1952 a self-taught RAF corporal, Derek Tipler, discovered some Welsh gypsies near Pwlhelli who spoke inflected Romani and claimed to be great-nephews of Llewellyn Wood, the harpist. Tipler had never seen the Rai's dictionary, but he did assemble six notebooks of Romani words. Alerted by Dora, Henry Francis of the Gypsy Lore Society went with him to Pwlhelli, but the birds had flown. For a time Tipler seemed a wonderful new source but, like a gypsy, he kept on disappearing until in 1957 he was discovered to be in Swansea prison for stealing a car.

Dora's chief link with the Rai was now Augustus John. He offended her when his autobiography *Chiaroscuro*, published in 1952, described the Rai's womanizing, but he explained that a second volume would make clear the Rai's deeper interest in gypsies. (Published posthumously, in 1964, *Finishing Touches* did not.) Nonetheless, the two continued to correspond about their campaigns, John describing his battle against his rural district council at Fordingbridge which had decided to 'civilise the Gypsies'.

In 1955, at the age of 75, Dora finally became editor of the Gypsy Lore Society Journal. John was her lifeline, keeping her in touch with gypsy friends including Clifford Lee and Dominic Reeve who camped in his grounds at Fordingbridge. Augustus painted a portrait of Clifford whose grandfather Ithal had carried the Rai's ashes up Foel Goch, and Dominic produced a well-reviewed book about gypsy life called *No Place Like Home* in 1960, with an introduction by John.

Augustus John remained loyal to the gypsies to the end. In November 1959 he told Dora: 'If my contacts with the Gypsies are less frequent than of old, they are, I find, no less cordial and rewarding.' When he died in 1961, Clifford Lee came down from Liverpool to pay homage at his gravestone at Fordingbridge, carrying a rose picked from the hedgerow: 'here is a wild rose from a wild man'. Dora was now still more alone, but she remained indomitable: when R. A. R. Wade, a much younger authority on gypsies, visited her he realized that 'we had been together for ten hours and the conversation had never stopped'. Though now more confused, she continued to edit the Journal with the tactful assistance of helpers.

When Dora died in 1973 at the age of 93, both the Journal and some of the old zeal for gypsy lore died with her. The Journal was soon revived in the same year as a fourth series by another group of enthusiasts, under the editorship of David Smith and with American financial help mobilized by the publisher Victor Weybright. But it now had a more political and practical perspective, reflecting fundamental changes in the gypsies' world. 'Their emergence as a problem group in urban society', wrote the new editor, 'is a matter that has attracted increased administrative, political and sociological attention.' There were still articles on Romani grammar and vocabularies, but also reviews of sociological and political books, including a study of gypsies and government policy and a Fabian pamphlet: 'Gypsies: Where Now?' The sense of the open road or the wind on the heath was fading.

Dora took many of our family secrets with her to the grave. She was, nevertheless, a conscientious librarian with a respect for the truth. In the recesses of the Liverpool University library she filed away the evidence which would explain some of our family puzzles.

13

The Aunt's Story

A FEW DAYS after the Rai's funeral in 1931 a mysterious woman arrived to spend a day at our house in Hampstead. She was introduced to me, aged 5, and my sister Dorothy, aged 7, as 'Aunt Mary' (my brother John was only a year old). She was a large, clumsy, short-sighted woman of 26, with shapeless clothes and a precise Scots voice. She seemed the ultimate schoolmarm. But she was very friendly, and we liked her. Dorothy was surprised to notice her weeping. After she left Dorothy received occasional postcards from her which delighted my sister but puzzled her: 'She was only here one day, Mummy, isn't it kind of her?'

Later, when I asked how Aunt Mary fitted in with Aunt Honor or Uncle Jack, my mother would not tell me, which of course whetted my curiosity. It was not until sixty years later that I was able to untangle the story. This – I discovered – was what had been happening among the grown-ups.

After the Rai died, my father was told that he had a half-sister who was the Rai's illegitimate daughter. How he was told we never knew, but for such an upright and shy man the relevation must have been traumatic. My father went up to see her in Edinburgh, where she was a schoolteacher, living alone on a pittance: for her mother – whoever she was – had also recently died. What Mary said to her half-brother, how they greeted each other, we never knew. But over the years it became clear that my father could not really face up to her problems: it was my mother who was to bear most of the burden.

The shock was greater still for my grandmother Margaret, who apparently had had no inkling of Mary's existence. However much she knew about the Rai's womanizing, this sudden revelation cast a shadow over all their past relationship. Was this why the Rai had spent weekends in Liverpool, and holidays apparently alone? Was this why he was so broke? My grandmother was devastated: she did not want to see Mary or hear anything about her.

Soon afterwards Mary came south to be interviewed for a new job at a school in London, and my mother invited her to Hampstead. It was hardly surprising that she was on that day distraught and weeping, for she had lost both her parents within the space of three months, and now faced for the first time her late father's legitimate family. But my mother was always kind-hearted and she befriended her with wonderful patience, though taking care not to tell her mother-in-law. My father was just off to Shanghai, to inspect chemical prospects in China on behalf of ICI: so he left the problem with my mother, and also with his Aunt Alice, the Rai's sister, who lived in Hastings and whom my mother asked to write to Mary.

Mary was soon due to come down to London again, to

apply for another possible post at Blackheath – near where her half-sister Honor was living with her husband Jack. Worried at the inevitable difficulties such proximity would cause, my father wrote to my mother from Shanghai in April 1932:

> Certainly it will be a bit difficult to keep her and Honor safely apart if she gets a job at Blackheath, but it can't be helped. The children will be a difficulty: they liked her and may talk about her. I can't think what to do about it. Of course they would be thrilled to be let into the secret but I think we could hardly do that, even to such a modern-educated child as Anthony. We shall just have to risk what they say and keep her an indefinite Aunt Mary.

Mary told Great-Aunt Alice that she was coming and was invited to stay for the weekend, for Alice knew that Mary was very poor and reckoned that she was 'perhaps the one most wronged by the selfishness of others'. My mother asked Mary to tea, though not to stay. Somehow my grandmother got to know of the visit and, hurt and angry, accused both Alice and my mother of conspiring against her.

Alice was equally hurt by Margaret's distrust of her: 'I had nothing whatever to do with Mary's visit to Hampstead that Sunday ... She is, as you point out, my niece, but it is not a relationship I have anything but pain in thinking about.' She sympathized with Margaret's agony but 'God knows I have suffered too at the amount of suffering and unhappiness you have had to bear.' My grandmother became more conciliatory, asking forgiveness, and Alice replied to 'my own dear Meg':

I don't feel there is anything to forgive ... I am quite, quite sure that there is not any such 'plan of secrecy' as you think. What has any one of us got to conceal? ... Why make yourself so very unhappy about what is really a trifle, and which need never be repeated ... you were so brave in facing it when it was there: surely you can try and turn you thoughts from it now.

My mother also assured my grandmother that she had no secret plan with Alice. Since Margaret had not wanted to talk or hear about Mary, she explained, 'Michael had decided it was pointless you knowing of her visit here ... Michael realized as much as I did what you had been through ... You must try and forgive us.'

The row was patched up. My mother became a dutiful prop to my grandmother, who moved to a bedsitter in Hampstead, and she also continued to befriend Aunt Mary, though often exhausted by her enthusing over the classics and ancient Greece as she hovered around the kitchen. My father remained aloof from his half-sister. After his return from China Dora corresponded with him about Mary, who had moved to a new teaching post. When Dora learnt that Mary Arnold had been upset by Scott Macfie's obituary, blaming Dora for it, she wrote to my father: 'Perhaps you can soothe MA when you do see her.'

We children only knew her as Aunt Mary, and the mystery which surrounded her made her seem all the more exciting. She came to stay with us on holiday in Dorset and it was there that we first got to know her better. She was still a strange being, with her ungainly movements, pebble glasses and lumbering walk, but she was full of energy, bringing a gust of the 'wind on the heath' into our lives. She strode with us over the Purbeck Downs; she taught us chess and played bagatelle; she was full of passionate knowledge and gave me a copy of Routledge's *Universal Encyclopaedia* which I still have by my desk. And she remembered our birthdays.

When I was about 18 my mother told me what I had already assumed. I could not understand what all the fuss was about. Soon afterwards I found myself based near Edinburgh as a midshipman in the Navy and visited Mary, who was teaching there, quite frequently, climbing up to the top of her tenement building in Lauriston Place. She was always welcoming and I felt no embarrassment. She would refer to the Rai with admiration and devotion, as my father never did, and sometimes gave me little treasures from him. With her big head and chin and strong build she looked more like the Rai than my father or any of the rest of us. She had also inherited his scholarly mind, his love of books and his pedantry, qualities which must have made her a formidable teacher. Even her handwriting resembled his. It later dawned on me that the Rai had loved her more than any of his legitimate children, but it was clear that she did not want to talk much about her life, past or present.

My father remained reticent about both Mary and his own early life. I realize now that he must always have felt very insecure. His father's poverty and Bohemian style had left him unsure about his own identity and had instilled in him a great need to conform, whether in the army or in the company for which he worked for most of his life. He had a horror of any demonstrative outburst – no doubt from witnessing his father's temper and heavy drinking – which would make him 'roll up like a hedgehog'. My sister, who was more observant than I, noticed that when he saw a drunk approaching in the street he would quickly try to divert us.

It was only when he was dying of cancer, at the age of

60, that he began to talk to me more freely. I had just returned from South Africa, had joined *The Observer* and had written my first book, *Drum*, which to my relief he had enjoyed – 'by Jove, it's *interesting*' – and which made him happier about my choice of profession. I brought my friend Father Huddleston from South Africa to see him. Though an atheist, my father welcomed him, and he in turn prayed for my father. A few weeks before he died he told me more about his father's family and friends, including Augustus John, but still said nothing about Mary. Mary herself came to pay her last respects to her half-brother; but the silence prevailed. My father died bravely, watching the trees swaying outside his window. 'At least I'm not afraid of the after-life,' he told me, 'I know it doesn't exist.' But he was still afraid of telling me the family secrets.

Mary continued to be sustained by the love of her father, and she decided to write her own biography of him, encouraged by Dora who plied her with advice and contacts, and who enjoyed discussing the old days with the Rai. 'I had been starved of Sampsonian news for over twenty years,' she told Mary after a weekend of reminiscence. Later she asked to look at some letters 'so that I too can enjoy the thrill of reading one or two items in the Rai's handwriting'.

But Mary's quest soon ran into painful discoveries. Dora urged her to interview Thomas Harkness Graham who had been the Rai's assistant in the early days of the university library. Mary went to see Graham, explaining that she had known the Rai from her student days at Manchester. She found him animated and very forthcoming, his words tumbling out. But his story was devastating, as Mary related to Dora:

he frankly told me that he loathed the Rai and gave his

reasons in no uncertain language. He told me all about what he called the 'philandering' in the Rai's room at the Library, beginning with Eileen Lyster and mentioning the affair with GMI [Damaris] and how May Allan had complained to the Vice Chancellor . . . I hadn't told him who I was and I don't think it was aimed at me though it may have been tentative fishing . . .

He told me how he used to take Michael out for walks and his sympathies were obviously all on Mrs Sampson's side. So you see it's no use sparing my feelings – I've got to face the facts and try to assess them justly. Shakespeare gave Romeo even a lady love before Juliet.

Dora was appalled that Mary had picked up such unpleasant impressions of the Rai and now had second thoughts about the whole project.

It is a very unhappy thing for your biography – because you are apparently collecting nothing but one-sided impressions of the Rai as University Librarian. I am deeply distressed about this, and am beginning to wonder if your *Life* will give a TRUE picture of J.S. after all!

Mary apparently calmed down and Dora encouraged her to conduct further interviews with friends of the Rai, including Augustus John – 'a very difficult man to deal with'. Mary wrote to John, explaining who she was. John mislaid the letter, but when he found it months later he was baffled: for although he had illegitimate children of his own, he had had no idea of Mary's existence. He wrote to Dora:

It is signed *Mary Arnold* and purports to be from a

daughter of John Sampson, whose life she is about to write, and asks for material. *Kon si-li?* [Who is she?] Never heard of this one.

What did he mean by 'this one'? Were there other illegitimate children he *did* know about? In any event, he agreed to see Mary, and wrote to her describing adventures with the Rai, and how they had both visited The Pines to call on Swinburne's companion, Theodore Watts-Dunton, and to try to see the poet himself. Dora apparently also wrote John a letter which has tantalizingly disappeared but which must have explained how Mary had come about and which stressed that it must be kept *garado* (secret). John replied: 'Your letter will be strictly *garado* . . . The Rai kept that secret well.'

That secrecy marked the limits of the Rai's Bohemia: he did not dare tell his fellow Bohemian about his much-loved daughter. Aunt Mary's interview with John is not recorded, but her biography did not progress far after that. And much later she came across a more worrying clue to her father's philandering. In April 1974 she received a letter from Helen Murray, a close friend of the Rai's rival Bernard Gilliat-Smith. She had been in touch with F. G. Huth, a gypsy expert who spoke the pure Romani. Huth had 'told Bernard that Dr Sampson had a son by a Gypsy girl who was brought up by the Gypsies, Dr S paying for his education.' Mary kept Helen Murray's letter but the search for my gypsy cousin has continued to frustrate me.

Much later, after both my parents had died and I had children of my own, I inherited the responsibility for Aunt Mary and provided her with a flat in Edinburgh. Mary would join us on expeditions through the Lowlands, enthusing about the glories of Scott, Burns or Ossian. Visiting us in London she seemed more at ease with her great-nieces and great-nephews who carried no burden of guilty secrets. One day, striding through Richmond Park, she quite suddenly began to talk more freely about her time with the Rai and gave a first glimpse of my grand-father's bigamous life: how she and her mother spent sum-mer holidays with him, unknown to the rest of the family or the university. Then she clammed up again. Afterwards in Edinburgh she talked about the Rai in a more academic vein, mentioning her biography but stressing that she would write it impersonally, in the third person: she seemed in no hurry to finish it.

In between my own journalistic adventures I remained tantalized. Who was Mary's mother? How did she fit in with the gypsies? And how could she have concealed her daughter's existence? As I grew older I became more curi-ous. By the spring of 1990, feeling more relaxed and reflec-tive after a heart operation, I set off on my own quest into the family past.

Aunt Mary was now 84, still living alone in her austere Edinburgh flat. She had countenanced no modernization: no refrigerator, no central heating, and no improvements to the ancient gas stove. 'I'm the original cave woman.' But she treated her books as dear friends who liked to be next to each other – Shelley next to Byron, Wordsworth to Coleridge – though they overflowed from the bookcases on to the floor. Her eyes were troublesome but she still read the *Aeneid* with the Classical Association. She said that this Indian summer was the happiest time of her life and she was fiercely proud of her independence, scorning her elderly friends who had retreated into nursing homes. She enjoyed my newspaper articles, though shocked by my woolly thinking. When I produced a light-hearted piece mentioning the mottos on the pound coin, she wrote (but did not send) a stern reproof: 'Your grandfather would have given you short shrift if he had found you describing a quotation from Virgil as mumbo jumbo.'

Once she suddenly said to me: 'You look so like the Rai.' This prompted me to ask casually about the gypsies. She explained that her mother had learnt and spoke Romani and had helped the Rai with his dictionary. Mary herself had known many of the gypsies, including Rosie Griffiths, and had learnt a few gypsy phrases including the words for whisky and 'I'm a Gypsy girl'. But, she added anxiously, 'that was not true – look at my blue eyes'. She paused: 'I felt rather awkward with the gypsies . . . You see I was rather conventional.' She had not been allowed to go to the Rai's funeral, she explained, because the others did not know she existed. 'Wasn't that a very hard time for you?' I asked. 'It was one of those times you have to go through.' She spoke calmly without a quiver of self-pity but would be drawn no further: 'I've talked enough.'

I decided to go to Liverpool to search for more clues among the city's ghosts. Not a ship was to be seen on the Mersey. The gypsy pubs in the docks had disappeared. The Adelphi Hotel had been refurbished with shiny bars and a night-club. Chatham Street, where the Bohemian scholars once congregated, had deteriorated into a slum. But the long decline had left many Victorian palazzi intact and I could still visualize that heyday of civic pride and intellectual adventure. And the entrance hall of the university was still dominated by a plaque commemorating in Latin its first librarian, John Sampson.

In the cellar of the new library block I found the Sampson archive, with rows of cardboard boxes full of white envelopes. For days I sat at a table while the friendly librarian with a shy deadpan expression brought more and more boxes from the shelves. The files must have been assembled by Dora Yates when she worked in the library;

and she had included not only the Rai's doggerel pornography but also her own bawdy verses – as though she were deliberately laying a trail.

In one envelope was a tantalizing note written in 1928, when the Rai was retiring from the library at Liverpool, which began 'Dearest' and ended 'Damaris'. A postscript referred to finding a house in Shrewsbury and was mysteriously signed 'Her Who'.

Damaris was the gypsy name which the Rai had given to Gladys Imlach, one of his four disciples, whose real name they both disliked. But why the signature 'Her Who'? Then I suddenly recalled the Rai's mock dedication of his dictionary:

To her who is my right-hand man
And eke my left leg girl.

So was it Damaris, not Dora, who was the Rai's favoured lover? The envelopes produced a further clue: the letter from Augustus John asking Dora about the mysterious Mary Arnold who claimed to be the Rai's daughter; followed by another letter thanking Dora for her *'garado'* explanation, which was not in the files.

From Liverpool I followed the trail to the Augustus John archive which had recently been bought by the University of Wales for its magnificent library which dominates Aberystwyth. There I found exuberant letters between the Rai and John, full of plans and stories about gypsies, some of them in Romani, with no sign of Dora's *'garado'* letter. But there was a letter to Dora from John's mistress Dorelia, enclosing a drawing of the Rai which stared out from the file. To reproduce it, I needed the permission of Vivien John, Augustus's daughter and executrix, who turned out to be a neighbour in London. She reminisced about her father and my grandfather and relished our family mystery. She described how Augustus's legitimate and illegitimate children had got on well together but added, 'my father could be surprisingly discreet'.

Mary's mother remained a mystery. Then I heard about a little Romani museum at Selborne in Hampshire. My wife and I found it in some huts on the edge of the village, surrounded by magnificent old gypsy caravans. I was greeted by the owner Peter Ingram, a handsome man with a shock of grey hair: 'So you're the Rai's grandson.' He was too young to have known the Rai himself, but he knew much about him and his museum contained many of his relics including the dictionary and photographs of his gypsy friends. Peter gave us tea in the immaculate small shed he had built in the yard, lined with decorated fittings like a gypsy caravan. He showed us his fine library of books about gypsies. Had he heard of *Freda's Fortune* by someone called Gladys Imlach? I asked. He reached up to a shelf and pulled out a book with a brightly embossed binding, which he had only recently bought through a catalogue. We skimmed through the sentimental illustrations and were about to dismiss it when we noticed the dedication: 'To Mary'. Beside it was a bookplate: *Ex Libris* Mary Arnold.

It was conclusive. Gladys or Damaris was Mary's mother. She must have dedicated the book to her daughter when she was a baby, and she in turn had only recently sold it. Peter was puzzled by my fascination. I explained that it solved a family secret. He laughed: 'I know about those kind of secrets. We call them "affairs of little Egypt".'

What kind of secret existence had Mary had as a child with her mother, cut off from her father's friends? She clearly had no wish to talk about it as she passed her eighties in dignity and contentment. She remained obstinately independent, surviving drastic operations and fixing her willpower on returning to her flat and her books. When, finally, at the age of 87 she realized she could no longer do so she died in her sleep at the hospital.

'Damaris' or Gladys Imlach, 1904

My sister and I went up to the memorial service at St Giles' Cathedral. There for the first time we saw the extent of her Edinburgh friendships and her closeness to the cathedral. The service was led by the minister and assisted by two other ministers while the great organ was played by her friend Heric Bunney. The central aisle filled up with fellow scholars, schoolteachers, members of literary societies and young people. The austere service ended with an address about Mary's rare combination of scholarship and friendship. At the cathedral door we met for the first time her friends who were clearly puzzled as to where these two Londoners fitted in. The committal service in the small bare chapel near the waters of Leith ended with an epistle from Horace: 'Give me my books'. Her friends in the Classical Association planned a 'Mary Arnold Memorial Lecture'.

The next day at Mary's flat we sorted out the piles of old cuttings, brochures and postcards which recorded every holiday and which overflowed the drawers and cupboards. There were books about Borrow, gypsies and Blake but no evidence of Mary's past life with the Rai. Had she obliterated every clue, even in the privacy of her own flat, to the father whom she had adored?

At last in the most inaccessible corner, in a narrow cupboard jammed behind the bedhead, I discovered a shabby envelope marked simply 'Rai'. It contained only a few letters and poems but enough to reveal the extent of her father's love that had kept her going through her hardships. Piecing them together with notebooks and other clues I could now finally assemble some picture of that bigamous life.

Mary's birth certificate showed that she had been born on 1 July 1906, when her mother was 26 and her father 44, at Littleborough, near Rochdale. Her father was registered as John Arnold (presumably in homage to 'The Scholar Gypsy'), and his profession as 'artist–painter' (his first ambition), while her mother was Gladys Maud Arnold. The Rai could only make fleeting visits from Liverpool but Dora and Eileen Lyster already knew about his baby. 'Oh my dear, it seems extraordinary that you should have been last week, almost incredible,' Damaris wrote to him soon after the birth. 'Dear, what are you doing? I want to know.

Somehow I feel cut off. Eileen said I could write as often as I liked, but I fancied I was wrong.'

A little later Damaris wrote again: 'I wish you could see your kid. She's getting so human and intelligent. All the people here say: "She's not like you Mrs Arnold, but very like your husband".' The Rai replied: 'I want to see my daughtie, and much more to see you . . . I have written to say I am not going away. I don't think I could now.'

When Mary was 3, Damaris got a job as a teacher at the Liverpool Institute High School for Girls on a very small salary. This was just at the time when the Rai was installing Margaret at his new home at Cae Gwyn in Wales, so he could visit Damaris and his daughter in term-time pro-vided his university colleagues did not see him. Only a few knew about Mary's existence, including Walter Raleigh and Mary Dowdall, 'the Rani', but not 'Kish' – she was not trusted with the secret until later.

The following year Mary and her mother moved into a house in Wavertree, near the school: 89 Gainsborough Road. The Rai wrote a poem about it. As with many biga-mists, his second life was cosily domestic, a love-nest with none of the wildness of Bohemia:

> And while she braved the damp, the dust,
> Belated Bone, and Shrivelled Crust,
> (Bearing it all without one moan)
> Dreamt of Possessions of Her Own,
> Of fair strange Plates, and Pots and Pans,
> Of pearly Kettles, Cups and Cans,
> Till she might found this blest Abode
> At nine and eighty Gainsborough Road.

At about this time Mary was sent to Edinburgh, where she was brought up by Damaris's sister Isabel who had two children of her own. Mary grew to love the city, and was happy and hard-working at school. She evidently only saw her father in the holidays, mostly in summer when they stayed in remote country villages in Yorkshire or Cumberland where no university colleague was likely to appear. Damaris left behind no correspondence from the Rai, only a few passionate poems.

By the time Mary was 11 she must have begun to show concern about her identity, for the Rai wrote a poem clearly addressed to her:

> Mother, who are you?
>   'The Lass who loved your father,
> And to him was true,
>   Him more than good name loved rather.'
>
> Who is my father, then?
>   'The man who loved your mother
> And in his weal and pain
>   Throned her high above every other.'
>
> And, mother, who am I?
>   'You are all that we gave you,
> As in floods hopelessly
>   We plunged to save you.'
>
> 'You are love, joy, despair,
>   Strength, frailty, passion,
> The seas that us upbear
>   The rocks we dash on.'
>
> 'You are our hope and good
>   No empire aimless,
> You are our flesh and blood,
>   Named or nameless.'

A year later Damaris moved within Wavertree to Blenheim House. There the Rai presided over a house-warming party which included Dora. A gypsy dinner was served with the menu in Romani. As the Rai put it:

> Caesar the fateful Rubicon has passed;
> Nelson has nailed his bunting to the mast,
>   But here on Blenheim's field
> Damaris, once more, her die has boldly cast . . .

Damaris rejoiced in the domestic peace:

> From out my low warm bed I rise
> To gaze around with happy eyes;
> The white cat steals along the bough;
> The black cat grins, "Tis morning now!'
> The kitten purrs, the puffin prances;
> Gay gleam the books and my heart dances . . .

But she also had more literary ambitions: she wrote a novel, *The Changing Years,* about a girl who escapes from her conventional father, marries a gypsy, has a child by him, falls in love with a painter, and ends up as a feminist. The publisher objected to the title, the weak beginning, the dialogue and the main character; and the novel never appeared in print.

At 13 Mary left Edinburgh for Liverpool to attend the same school where her mother was teaching. The move was not a happy one, for she never felt close to her mother. 'The best thing about her', she once told my sister, 'was her wonderful speaking voice, when she read me stories.' No one was supposed to know that they were related. At school her mother was not Mrs Arnold but Miss Imlach. The isolation of Mary's life is almost unimaginable. She had a room in the attic: and if she was downstairs when the front doorbell rang she had to pick up any belongings and rush up upstairs before the door was opened. When she went to school she left at a different time, by the back door.

Her summer holidays were very happy times, bathed in the love of her father. He helped her with two issues of the 'Blenheim Magazine', including one for her thirteenth birthday with a triolet from Dora:

> Have you heard the news?
>   Mary's just thirteen.
>
> Help me out, O Muse!
> Have you heard the news?
> Let me pay my dues
>   To this birthday queen.
> Have you heard the news?
>   Mary's just thirteen.

The Rai was at that point finally separating from Margaret and could now spend more time in Damaris's house in Wavertree which he evidently regarded as his own. 'How do you like our new letter-paper stamp?' he wrote to Mary from Blenheim House. 'I hope you feel duly flattered at being the first person it has ever been used for.' When Mary was preparing for her School Certificate examination, the Rai composed an 'Ode to a Young Lady on her Sixteenth Birthday'.

> You were a beamish babe when young,
> Our bread upon the waters flung
>   Which, after many days
> Returned with interest, so to speak,

> To edify our lonely creek
> To floriate our angles bleak
>   And irrigate our ways.
>
> We wish you joy in your exams,
> And may there be no jars or jams –
>   Though jars of jam may be . . .

The next year she won a scholarship to Manchester University, excelling in her Latin papers, which overjoyed the Rai: 'You can imagine my delight and excitement this morning and wild desire to think and talk of nothing else . . .' 'Gorgeous news,' he wrote again a week later, 'I commend, laud, bepraise, applaud, cheer, panegyrize, eulogize, extol, glorify, magnify and exalt. So will Damaris! . . . Classics *is* a better subject than lit., that I've always felt, *really severer* and *stronger*.'

Mary prospered at Manchester University. She told the Rai that her professor had said her Latin prose was first class, a pleasure to correct. But she was slightly worried by a book that the Rai had sent her, which described him as being fond of 'low life'. 'Is it a thing to be proud of? I trust you will reassure me on the point.'

In the same year the Rai's dictionary was published. He did not celebrate it with his official family, but he presided over a gypsy feast for Damaris and her friends:

> Ladies, I rise to proffer you the toast
> Of her whose pretty spurred heel can boast
> It drave my Opus past the winning post.
>
> All that I know of love I learned from her.
> Pearl, onyx, chalcedony, camphor, myrrh,
> Asparagus, jasmine, lilai and ver.

Who is that girl? We all well wot I wis.
Who for us conjugated 'am', 'are', 'is'?
And Echo sweetly answers 'Damaris'.

When Mary received a second-class degree he avoided
recriminations – as he had not with my father. 'Dear, you
have done quite well! A first would have been just a shade
more delightful, but I hadn't been *building* on that.' She
took a job as a school-teacher and remained out of sight of
the Rai's friends even after he had retired. She sometimes
visited him in Shrewsbury and West Kirby, and he still
wrote loving letters. 'I never feel really prouder than when
the weekend arrives on which I don a pair of socks knit-
ted by you. The pride and exultation begins in my toes,
and creeps up swiftly to my brain where it lingers by virtue
of the faculty called Memory.'

My grandfather's last months remain shrouded. Mostly
he seems to have been alone, looked after by a housekeeper
and sometimes visited by Rosie Griffiths. In West Kirby he
was much closer to both Dora and Damaris who would
come to him on Thursdays and read letters from Mary 'in
a very special voice'. Sometimes Dora would come and dis-
cuss gypsy affairs and the Gypsy Lore Society which was
again in crisis, but the Rai was too ill to do much about it.
His heart and lungs were bad and he suffered from gout:
as he joked, *'chacun à son goût'*.

In August 1931 Damaris underwent an operation, and a
few days later she died. The school magazine recorded that
she had been there twenty-two years – 'a woman of fine
scholarship and strong personality' – but made no mention of her daughter.

Mary left few clues about her life during the bleak
months that followed. The Rai wrote six weeks after her
mother's death, urging a more frequent correspondence:

'Let's try and keep things going as best we may. Let it be yours to keep me up to the mark. Remember I am a frail man.' He had been cheered by driving to North Wales with Rosie Griffiths and her mouth-organ, revisiting old haunts: 'Every tree, stone and stick recalled some adventure (of no importance whatever) to delighted Rozi.'

Two weeks later he related a story about Rosie spilling gravy over Dora's copy of *Punch*. Early in November he was complaining about the honorary degrees at Liverpool including one awarded to Eleanor Rathbone, 'fussy and self-important'. Rosie had just paid another visit: 'she runs about a bright spot of colour, rejoicing in her small missions and executing some of them quite well'. A few days later he was reassuring Mary: 'I am making a spirited attempt to recover my normal health.' Within hours he was dead.

Having lost her mother three months before, Mary had now lost the father whom she adored more than anyone. She was excluded from his funeral because her existence was not known. Only the gypsies could console her. Just after the funeral Jim Wood, who had married Bessie Goldsach, wrote to Dora from Earlstown:

> Bessie and I received your letter this morning and we are very sorry indeed to hear of the Rai and Daia's deaths. Bessie cried when she read of Mary's distress. I reassured myself Miss Dora with the thought that, as long as you ... are alive, they will always have someone to succour her. What a beautiful thought that they are again united after so short a separation ...

He wrote again to thank Dora for a photograph of the Rai: 'I have an enlargement of Mary when she was quite little at Prestatyn, so I will frame the Rai's and hang them side by side.' Another of the Woods, Mary Hannah Winders, also wrote to Dora about the funeral:

I can't tell you how pleased I was to see you all at the funeral and also my dear relatives some of them I hadn't seen for 45 years, I am thinking of them all the time, I wouldn't have missed going if I had to walk it. Dear Dora I am very happy and proud to think that the dear Rye wished for us all to be there, and his kindness to us all will live for ever in our memory. We have all lost a dear kind friend.

I am writing to Mary now to tell her all that happened on Saturday and to tell her to get married and have some children.

Mary Hannah then wrote the promised letter to Mary, describing the funeral:

I suppose you will have read all about the ceremony at Foel Goch and I have got lots of pictures of it. The one enclosed is my daughter Kitty marked with a cross and you can just see my hat, I am behind my cousin Henry Wood. I have also enclosed a bit of the moss from just where the ashes were scattered. It is a beautiful mountain, just like a carpet of velvet covered with lovely green moss.

Yes dear, their hands and souls have met across the dark waters for ever. It was a beautiful ceremony and I wouldn't have missed it for anything. Their dear names will live for ever in the true hearts of the Gypsies. So I have tried to tell you all my dear, and when I see you I will tell you every little thing that happened.

Kamiben
Mary Hannah

The faded piece of moss still survived in a tiny envelope hidden in Mary's cupboard: her only keepsake of her father's funeral from which she had been excluded. Yet she could never feel close to the gypsies though they had been friends in her hour of need.

Mary never talked to any of us about that lonely ordeal. But she was strong. She had already been forged by self-reliance and self-denial, as we had not: 'all we can leave you is good health and a good brain', her parents had told her. She made the most of them as she carved out her own life as a teacher and scholar, and built up life-long friendships.

On the face of it, hers was a tragic story – the victim of hypocrisy and false morality, shut out from the family and the inheritance which was her right. But she was always realistic, never self-pitying: always confident in her brain and values, fortified by the memory of her father.

It was the legitimate family who were more confused by their inheritance from their missing paterfamilias. He had first dominated his children, pressing them to academic achievement and bravery in war, and then disappeared in a cloud of gypsy smoke into a bigamous life and another society, a contradiction which he could never resolve. When his own children discovered his double life they sought to bury it in silence. But his grandchildren and great-grandchildren had some recompense – a reminder that life can never be contained within the four walls of middle-class conventions, and that 'the other society' can never be ignored.

14

The Last of the Gypsies

WHAT HAS HAPPENED to the pure Romani language and the Wood family who spoke it? What is left of that wild gypsy dream which so enthralled intellectuals a century ago?

The Woods have certainly established a place in history. In 1991 Eldra Jarman, one of the clan, published with her husband *The Welsh Gypsies: Children of Abram Wood.* Eldra comes from the Roberts family of harpists who intermarried with the Woods: when she first played the harp at 14 a local journalist noted that 'her somewhat swarthy complexion marked her out as one of Abram Wood's descendants'. In their book the Jarmans describe how the two families gradually became more assimilated into British society as they moved out of their tents and barns to become 'house-Gypsies', as they married out of the gypsy tribes, and as they were dispersed by two world wars. By the late twentieth century, however, they were searching for their roots. 'Many of the descendants of both branches are evincing a powerful, indeed insatiable, curiosity about their origins and family history'. And the Jarmans look back to the Rai's dictionary as the guide to their language and folklore.

I visited them in their house outside Cardiff, its walls lined with books, a harp standing in the drawing-room. Eldra insists 'I am proper Romani first, Welsh second . . . Fred [her husband] kept me down when I wanted to fly.' Her family are proud of their dark looks, and all four grandchildren play the harp: one, a natural musician, turned down a university place to travel through Ireland playing and busking. Eldra speaks a few simple Romani words at home including *kial* (cheese), *gudlo* (sugar), *drom* (road), *jukel* (dog), *stadi* (hat) and *misto dosta* (very well). None of the family speak the pure Romani, but in their book they 'wonder whether the Welsh dialect of Romani is still alive somewhere in the hills and villages of northern Wales'.

Were there other Woods who had kept the language alive? I went back to Peter Ingram's gypsy museum. There he keeps track of Abram Wood's descendants and has a framed copy of the extended family tree through which my grandfather traced his progeny. He lamented how the old gypsy traditions had been debased and exploited by New Age travellers, and went through the names of Woods who had emigrated, disappeared or married into the towns: many of the best gypsy families were running profitable businesses, particularly in scrap-metal or carpets. But in North Wales he knew about grandchildren of Matthew Wood, who taught my grandfather the pure Romani.

So I went with my wife to the Rai's old haunts, among the lakes and mountains of North Wales. They are far less remote and mysterious than a century earlier: the main road to Holyhead is clogged with heavy trucks which dispel any air of romance. But the turning to Bettws-Gwerfil-Goch still looks like the 'road to nowhere', an unfenced lane twisting through sheep-cropped hills. The little village of low white houses seems timeless, and the austere house Cae Gwyn still stands at the top of the hill. Beyond Bettws there lies the hamlet of Llangwm, with a steep path winding along the stream up to the top of Foel Goch, the 'Red Mountain'.

We found the small church by the sea near Dolgellau, with the simple gravestone carved with the initials AW, where the patriarch of the tribe, Abram Wood, is buried. But we could find no clues among the locals about the surviving family or their language.

At Bala we sought out Matthew Wood's granddaughter, Alice Davies, and were directed to a nearby housing estate where we were welcomed by a handsome, dark-skinned woman and her husband Norman, a champion fly-fisher. Alice was 5 when my grandfather died, she explained, but she remembered it as if it were yesterday. 'They came home blind drunk after a wake in Llangwm.' Alice also has a hazy memory of her grandfather Matthew: 'They called him the mole – he would just disappear.' Like the Jarmans the Davies are now proud of their gypsy inheritance, particularly the music: Alice's father Manfri loved playing the fiddle, and her daughter is a keen violinist. But Alice insists she cannot speak a word of the pure Romani for it was bullied out of her at school. Being dark, she did not want to be different. 'It was the teachers more than the children – they would smack me on the face because I was a Gypsy.'

On a later visit Alice and Norman directed us to their cousin Matthew Wood, grandson of his namesake. He is based in a comfortable house opposite the old Bala chapel with his Filipina wife, but spends his days in the open air, fishing and shooting in the surrounding hills. He too said he could speak no deep Romani, though he remembered how his father talked it with his uncles. But Eldra Jarman later insisted that the Woods in Bala still keep Romani as their private language, and that Matthew had once boasted: 'I could bedazzle you.'

There were still other Woods. I had a letter out of the blue from Liverpool which was signed by a June Maguire, formerly June Wood. She had been investigating her ancestors in the Liverpool University library, she explained, when she suddenly realized they were gypsies. 'It was the shock of my life. I asked myself: what will the librarian think?' But as she learnt more about the Wood family she became prouder of them, particularly her great-grandmother Betsy Wood, the expert on gypsy customs and songs who had helped to educate the Rai. She had tracked down other members of the clan, and had organized a reunion at Newton-le-Willows to which twenty Woods came.

June invited me to a family lunch near Liverpool. Among the guests were two grandchildren of Betsy Wood together with Reubena Wood, a lively half-gypsy of 80, who is the eldest daughter of Jim Wood who had helped the Rai with his vocabulary and befriended his daughter Mary after her parents had died. Reubena gave me a vivid glimpse of my grandfather's other life as she had seen it as a child, when the Rai visited her parents with his other wife Damaris and their young daughter Mary. As a child Reubena was very shy, hiding under the table because she only wore clogs, but she never forgot the Rai: 'a big man, broader than you, wearing a hairy jacket'. Her father admired him but 'thought he was after my mum'. Reubena spent most of her later life in service in a big house, while remaining proud of her gypsy forebears: she interspersed her talk with a few Romani words, but she too had abandoned her father's language.

Soon afterwards came another gypsy invitation to Liverpool, from Sheila Lee, the widow of Clifford whose grandfather Ithal Lee had carried the Rai's ashes. I had tea with her, a bright-eyed woman of 73, surrounded by family pictures including a copy of Augustus John's portrait of her husband. Clifford had always respected Romani traditions: as a young couple they had travelled in a caravan, sometimes staying in John's garden. When Clifford died, Sheila burnt his clothes and smashed the crockery gypsy-fashion, to the delight of the children. And the family still say *jukel* for dog, *pande the woder* for shut the door, and *wafedo soom* (a bad smell – used to describe strange people at a gathering).

Sheila was proud of the academic achievements of her offspring, including a granddaughter teaching law at Oxford; but she was also proud of her Romani connections, and outraged by anti-gypsy outbursts from local councillors. She was very conscious that people who had once preferred to forget their gypsy blood were now keen to trace it. She had urged Clifford to research his antecedents, and their son Kenneth later took up the quest. A lecturer at the University of Newcastle in Australia, he started a Romani association which helped many families trace their ancestry. There is now a widespread longing for gypsy roots. As Sheila Lee explains it: 'When people are unsettled they grasp at straws. That's why they want to be Gypsies.'

The gypsy aristocrats – the Woods, the Lees and the Roberts – are themselves becoming more interested in their ancestry just as their customs and traditions are vanishing. The younger generation, now settling into suburban houses, look back with all the more longing to the memories of their nomadic life and proximity to nature which once made them unique.

The deep Romani language itself is now virtually extinct.

Throughout Europe the gypsies' traditional speech has become mixed up with local languages, to produce hybrids which vary increasingly between countries. In 1992, Sir Angus Fraser noted in his authoritative study, *The Gypsies*, 'Romani has become a network of perhaps sixty dialects, falling into a score of groupings ... It is indeed debatable whether Romani has not reached a stage where it should be considered as a group of closely related languages rather than as a single language with numerous dialects.' And the scholarly philological interest in gypsies and their culture has been overtaken in the 1990s by the more urgent political concern with their persecution and migration from Eastern Europe which still has the great majority of the gypsy population.

Across Europe there remain large gypsy communities quite separate from modern industrial society, resisting the encroachments of motorways, supermarkets and compulsory schools. The more materialist and competitive the rest of society, the more their resistance stands out, as they reject fixed possessions or regimented routines. And they still provide an awkward test, as they have for the last five centuries, of the tolerance of European societies and governments towards alternative life-styles and values.

The gypsy enchantment, promising an escape from the suffocation and drudgery of the cities, still works its spell among each new generation of non-gypsies – whether luring them to set off in convoys of battered buses and trucks as New Age travellers, or to establish rural communes in the hills, or to pursue Utopias among distant tribes in other continents, or simply vicariously to enjoy the wild dances or music which defy the ordered rational world. The old image of the gypsy seductress, of Carmen or Esmeralda beckoning men to their destruction, however tamed or vulgarized by films and musicals, still holds some power to 'madden men's minds' and to provoke defiance of all conventions. The lure of the camp-fire in the open countryside still expresses the longing to return to nature and the wind on the heath, and to make people wonder, as the Rai put it, whether 'Madam Civilization may not have put her money on the wrong horse'.

The gypsy wagon, too, still preserves some magic as the entrance into that mysterious world, despite its later degeneration into the mass-produced box on a municipal camp-site. Just as I was finishing this book I heard from Mervyn Jones, a friendly expert on gypsies in North Wales, that an old caravan called Esmeralda had just come up for sale near Macclesfield. It sounded very like the wagon in which the Rai had camped with his children near Bettws-Gwerfil-Goch, and which other enthusiasts of the Gypsy Lore Society had used on their sentimental journeys through the hills. I went up to inspect her with Mervyn:

Esmeralda, c. 1912

she stood in a front garden, a simple bow-topped wagon with a crooked chimney and small shuttered windows. Her canvas roof was leaking and her inside had collapsed, but she was unmistakably the same wagon which had featured in many sepia photographs of the scholar gypsies nearly a century ago. She was irresistible. Esmeralda will now stand restored to dignity in our Wiltshire garden as a testament to that mysterious dream.

Bibliography

PRIMARY SOURCES

The most valuable collection of letters and documents about gypsies and Romani scholarship is in the Gypsy Collection at Liverpool University, which includes archives devoted to John Sampson, Dora Yates and Scott Macfie, together with magnificent photographs of gypsies, caravans and camps by Fred Shaw and others.

The National Library of Wales contains the Augustus John Archive which includes letters between the artist and John Sampson.

The letters from John Sampson to his wife Margaret are held by my cousin Sally Stephen. The letters between John Sampson and his son Michael Sampson are in my possession.

SELECTED PUBLISHED SOURCES

The major book by John Sampson is his Romani dictionary: *The Dialect of the Gypsies of Wales* (Oxford, Clarendon Press, 1926). He also compiled an anthology of writings about gypsies: *The Wind on the Heath* (London, Chatto & Windus, 1930). His miscellaneous verse and contributions were collected by Dora Yates as *In Lighter Moments* (Liverpool, Liverpool University Press, 1934).

Dora Yates also wrote her own reminiscences, *My Gypsy Days* (London, Phoenix House, 1953). A short account of her life was provided by Elizabeth Bradburn, *Dr Dora Yates, An Appreciation* (Liverpool, Liverpool University Press, 1975). Other books by John Sampson's disciples are Eileen Lyster's *The Gypsy Life of Betsy Wood* (London, Dent, 1926) and G. M. Imlach's *Freda's Fortune* (London, T.C. and E.C. Jack, 1907).

More details about John Sampson and his relations with Augustus John are included in the revised biography of the artist by Michael Holroyd, *Augustus John: The New Biography* (London, Chatto & Windus, 1996). Lively episodes in their stormy friendship are included in the first volume of John's own memoir: *Chiaroscuro, Fragments of Autobiography* (London, Jonathan Cape, 1952). John's relationship with North Wales is described in the short commentary to the exhibition at Llandudno in 1982 by Eric Rowan: *Some Miraculous Promised Land* (Llandudno, Mostyn Art Gallery, 1982). There is also an informative booklet about the John Archive at the National Library of Wales, by Ceridwen Lloyd-Morgan, with insights into Sampson's influence on John.

Among the many studies of gypsy language and culture, the most relevant to this book are the volumes of the *Journal of the Gypsy Lore Society*, published from 1888 by T. A. Constable in Edinburgh, in four series with breaks between them. The *Journal* has now been revived with a fifth series published in the United States (5607 Greenleaf Road, Cheverly, Maryland 20785).

The extensive literature about George Borrow has a very useful addition in the *George Borrow Bulletin* published since 1991 by the George Borrow Society, and edited by Dr Ann Ridler from St Mary's Cottage, 61 Thame Road, Warborough, Wallingford, Oxon OX10 7EA.

Some of the books on gypsies which are most relevant to John Sampson's own writings are:

Francis Hindes Groome, *Gypsy Folk Tales* (London, Hurst Blackett, 1899);

George Hall, *The Gypsy's Parson* (London, Sampson Low, 1915);

C.G. Leland, *The Gypsies* (London, Trubner, 1882);

Andrew McCormick, *The Tinkler-Gypsies* (London, Simpkin Marshall, 1906);

Bob Skot (R.A. Scott Macfie), *A Brief Account of Gypsy History, Persecutions, Character and Customs* (Liverpool, Robert McGee, 1909); and

Brian Vesey-Fitzgerald, *Gypsies of Britain* (London, Chapman and Hall, 1944).

Details of the Shelta language, making much use of John Sampson's collections and manuscripts, are contained in R.A. Stewart MacAlister, *The Secret Languages of Ireland* (Cambridge, Cambridge University Press, 1937).

The most recent and authoritative survey of gypsy history and culture is by Angus Fraser, *The Gypsies* (Oxford, Blackwell, 1992).

The development of the Wood and Roberts families over the twentieth century has been chronicled by A.O.H. and Eldra Jarman, *The Welsh Gypsies* (Cardiff, University of Wales Press, 1991).

The problems and ordeals of gypsies during and since the Second World War are described and analysed by Donald Kenrick and Graham Putton, *The Destiny of Europe's Gypsies* (London, Chatto-Heinemann for Sussex University Press, 1972). Vivid descriptions and accounts of gypsies in contemporary Eastern Europe are contained in Isabel Fonseca, *Bury Me Standing* (London, Chatto & Windus, 1995).

I have also made use of several memoirs and descriptions of academic life earlier in the century, particularly in Liverpool, including:

John Gross, *The Rise and Fall of the Man of Letters* (London, 1969);

Thomas Kelly, *For Advancement of Learning* (Liverpool, Liverpool University Press, 1981);

Geoffrey Keynes, *The Gates of Memory* (Oxford, Clarendon Press, 1981);

Sean O. Luing, *Kuno Meyer* (Dublin, Geography Publications, 1991);

A Miscellany Presented to J.M. Mackay (Liverpool, Liverpool University Press, 1914);

Ramsay Muir, *An Autobiography* (London, Lund Humphries, 1943);

K. M. E. Murray, *Caught in the Web of Words* (Oxford, Oxford University Press, 1977);

Stephen Potter, *Muse in Chains* (London, 1937); and

C. H. Reilly, *Scaffolding in the Sky* (London, Routledge, 1938).

Acknowledgements

IN PURSUING THIS STORY I have owed much to old and new friends who have encouraged and helped me on the way and made the journey thoroughly enjoyable. My sister Dorothy Meade and my wife Sally have throughout shared the quest and added their own curiosity and discoveries. My cousins Sally Stephen and Joan Baxter have generously given me access to our grandfather's letters, and have encouraged me forward. Charles Elliott of Alfred Knopf first urged me to follow the trail, and offered shrewd suggestions. Sir Angus Fraser, always generous with his valuable time, has contributed precious documents and insights. Peter Ingram of the Romani museum in Selborne has often pointed me in the right direction. The late Vivien John, Augustus John's daughter, and Rebecca John, his granddaughter, have told me more about his relationship with my grandfather, and have allowed me to reproduce his pictures; while John's biographer Michael Holroyd has shared discoveries with me. Mervyn Jones has brought his own copious knowledge of gypsy lore to bear. Donald Kenrick has advised me about Continental gypsies and their history. Brian Raywid has led me to useful sources.

In Wales I was made especially welcome by members of the

Wood and Roberts families, whose gypsy forebears were my grandfather's friends, and they were forthcoming in their reminiscences and information. At Bala I was warmly received by two grandchildren of Matthew Wood, Alice Davies and the younger Matthew Wood. In Cardiff Eldra Jarman and her husband Professor Jarman, authors of *The Welsh Gypsies,* were wonderfully helpful.

In Liverpool Sheila Lee added very useful background about her husband's gypsy grandfather Ithal Lee and put me in touch with her son Kenneth at the University of Newcastle in Australia. Also in Liverpool June Maguire was marvellously hospitable and introduced me to other members of the Wood family.

I spent many happy hours in Liverpool. I am indebted to the library staff at the university for making available the papers of my grandfather and his friends, including Adrian Allen, assistant archivist, and particularly to the staff of the Special Collections, including Ian Jackson, J.R. Clegg and Katy Hooper. I was also helped by Janice Carpenter, Curator of the Art Collections at the university, and by Edward Morris, Curator of Fine Arts at the Walker Gallery. My friend Michael Harrison was generous with contributing research.

At the National Library of Wales at Aberystwyth I was guided by Ceridwen Lloyd-Morgan, who looks after the Augustus John Archive. I am also grateful to Professor Lisa Tickner of Middlesex University; Professor Ian Rogerson of the John Rylands Institute at Manchester; and Lord Bridges, grandson of the poet, for allowing access to John Sampson's letters to his grandfather.

I am indebted to Julius White, grandson of Augustus John, for permission to reproduce the paintings and drawings by the artist in this book – perpetuating the generosity of his grandfather to my grandfather. John's portrait of Kuno Meyer is reproduced courtesy of the National Gallery of Ireland.

I must also thank the Gypsy Collections of the University of Liverpool Library for permission to reproduce the photographs of John Sampson with his disciples, Esmeralda Lock, Matthew and Harry Wood, and gypsies at John Sampson's funeral.

Acknowledgements

The engraving of Esmeralda on p.28 is taken from Francis Hindes Groome's *In Gypsy Tents* (Edinburgh, Nimmo, 1880). The drawing of John Sampson on p.154 was executed from a photograph by Lawrence Wright, from *In Lighter Moments*, the anthology of John Sampson's writings (Liverpool, Liverpool University Press, 1934).

The engraving of Liverpool University College on p.43 and the photograph of Dora Yates on p.80 are taken from Elizabeth Bradburn, *Dr Dora Yates, An Appreciation* (Liverpool, Liverpool University Press, 1975). The caricature of John Sampson by Augustus John on p.133 and the drawing of 'Doonie' by her husband Albert Lipczinski on p.67 are reproduced courtesy of the University of Liverpool Art Gallery.

I am especially glad to be published by John Murray, the publishers of George Borrow who inspired my grandfather with his Victorian adventures. I have much appreciated the encouragement and interest of the managing director, Nicholas Perren, and the supportiveness and scrutiny of my editor Gail Pirkis. As with earlier books I could not do without the patient editing and transcribing of my assistant Carla Shimeld who has again produced some order out of chaos. And I am delighted that my friend Douglas Matthews, the former librarian of the London Library, has been able to compile the index with his usual thoroughness.

Anthony Sampson
London, October 1996

Index

Page numbers in *italic* indicate illustrations

Index

Index

Index

Index

Index